12.95

ARAGON
ISSUES IN
PHILOSOPHY

PARAGON ISSUES IN PHILOSOPHY

THE PARAGON ISSUES IN PHILOSOPHY SERIES

At colleges and universities, interest in the traditional areas of philosophy remains strong. Many new currents flow within them, too, but some of these—the rise of cognitive science, for example, or feminist philosophy—went largely unnoticed in undergraduate philosophy courses until the end of the 1980s. The Paragon Issues in Philosophy Series responds to both perennial and newly influential concerns by bringing together a team of able philosophers to address the fundamental issues in philosophy today and to outline the state of contemporary discussion about them.

More than twenty volumes are scheduled. They are organized into three major categories: The first covers the standard topics—metaphysics, theory of knowledge, ethics, and political philosophy—but these books stress innovative developments in those disciplines. The second focuses on more specialized but still vital concerns in the philosophies of science, religion, history, sport, and other areas. The third category explores new work that relates philosophy and fields such as feminist criticism, medicine, economics, technology, and literature.

The level of writing is aimed at undergraduate students who have little previous experience studying philosophy. The books provide brief but accurate introductions that appraise the "state of the art" in their fields and show how the history of thought about their topics developed. Each volume is complete in itself but also complements others in the series.

Traumatic change characterizes these last years of the 20th century—all of it involves philosophical issues. The philosophy editor for Paragon House, Don Fehr, has worked with us to develop this series. We hope it will encourage the understanding needed in our times, which are as complicated and problematic as they are promising.

John K. Roth   Frederick Sontag
Claremont McKenna College   Pomona College

LIVING THE
GOOD LIFE

ALSO BY GORDON GRAHAM

Historical Explanation Reconsidered, 1983

Politics in Its Place: A Study of Six Ideologies, 1986

Contemporary Social Philosophy, 1988

The Idea of Christian Charity: A Critique of Some Contemporary Conceptions, 1990

GORDON GRAHAM

UNIVERSITY OF ST. ANDREWS,
SCOTLAND

LIVING THE GOOD LIFE: AN INTRODUCTION TO MORAL PHILOSOPHY

PARAGON ISSUES IN PHILOSOPHY

PARAGON HOUSE · NEW YORK

FIRST EDITION, 1990

PUBLISHED IN THE UNITED STATES BY PARAGON HOUSE

PARAGON HOUSE
90 FIFTH AVENUE
NEW YORK, NY 10011

COPYRIGHT © 1990 BY PARAGON HOUSE

SERIES DESIGNED BY KATHY KIKKERT

LIBRARY OF CONGRESS CATALOGING-IN-PUBLICATION DATA

GRAHAM, GORDON.
    LIVING THE GOOD LIFE : AN INTRODUCTION TO MORAL
PHILOSOPHY / GORDON GRAHAM. — 1ST ED.
        P.   CM.
    INCLUDES BIBLIOGRAPHICAL REFERENCES.
    ISBN 1-55778-235-0
    1. ETHICS.   I. TITLE.
    BJ1025.G68   1990 C. 2
    171—DC20   90-30106
                                                              CIP

THE PAPER USED IN THIS PUBLICATION MEETS THE MINIMUM
REQUIREMENTS OF AMERICAN NATIONAL STANDARD FOR
INFORMATION SCIENCES—PERMANENCE OF PAPER FOR PRINTED
LIBRARY MATERIALS, ANSI Z39.48-1984.

MANUFACTURED IN THE UNITED STATES OF AMERICA
10 9 8 7 6 5 4 3 2 1

CONTENTS

ACKNOWLEDGMENTS

My understanding of the issues dealt with in this book has benefited greatly over a number of years from discussions with colleagues and students. I am especially grateful, however, to the editors of this series, John K. Roth and Frederick Sontag, and to my colleagues Hugh Upton and Anthony Ellis (now of Virginia Commonwealth University) for copious comments on the typescript. I know that they have saved me from many errors of substance and presentation. I am also indebted to Eve Poole for giving me the most important sort of view, that of the newcomer to philosophy.

St Andrews, December 1989

Introduction:
How to Use This Book

■t is not easy to introduce people to the study of philosophy.
Onc major difficulty is that there is no body of fact or theory
that comprises 'the subject' and which is there waiting to be
learned. Indeed, philosophy is not really a *subject* at all, but
an activity. It is something we learn to *do* rather than something
we come to *know*. It is not a body of knowledge so much as a
way of thinking. This does not mean that philosophy has no
topics of its own. It is true that philosophers sometimes make
their contribution to human understanding by thinking in a
distinctive manner about subjects that historians or scientists
also discuss. But there are some topics that can only be thought
about in a philosophical manner—for instance, the nature of
reality itself, the proof (if any) of God's existence, the relation
of the mind and the body, the foundations of good and evil.
These are the special topics of philosophy because only philosophical thinking can improve our understanding of them.

One of these topics, the nature of good and evil, provides
the principal subject of this book. Before we begin the discussion proper, however, something more needs to be said about
the nature of philosophical thinking and the best way to use
this book. Since the time of Socrates, five hundred years before
Christ, dialectical argument has been an important philosophical method. This is argument that proceeds from claim to
counterclaim, thesis to counterthesis, testing every point critically as it goes. The test consists in drawing out the implications

of each claim that is made and examining these implications for consistency with all the other elements in the argument. Dialectical argument is not merely assertion and counterassertion of opinion, but a process in which thought is clarified, made more precise, and given a rational grounding.

Dialectical argument is not the only method of thought and inquiry that has figured in the history of philosophy, but in many ways it is the most impressive. This is because it demands a high level mental organization and critical detachment. It both requires and produces rigorous intellectual discipline. Those who want to learn how to do philosophy in this way must first of all abandon the inclination merely to give vent to personal opinion, or speculatively develop a personal point of view. Neither of these practices is philosophy, though there is a common inclination to do both among those who talk about moral matters. Rather, dialectical philosophy consists in putting our own opinions and those of others to the most critical test we can.

This book employs the method of dialectical argument. In each chapter a thesis is examined and refined by a process of dialectical thought that moves back and forth. Sometimes this process can seem confusing, and at times it may take a special effort to follow all the twists and turns of the argument. In the course of this argument, the writings of many famous philosophers are drawn upon, but only as they relate to the line of thought that is being pursued. There is no attempt here to expound systematically the ideas of historical figures in chronological order. This may give the appearance that the ideas of these philosophers are being made secondary to advancing the author's own ideas. But one important implication of the choice of the dialectical method is that the arguments presented in this book are not there to be learnt and repeated, still less simply accepted, but to be examined critically. What this book attempts to do is to introduce philosophy by engaging you in argument. The mark of its success lies not in your coming to share a certain view, but in your taking up the argument for yourself.

There are three important steps to follow in mastering and examining the material in this book.

1. First, having read the arguments of a particular section, see if you can set down on paper the main points in a connected sequence. This exercise will give you practice at arranging your own thoughts in a logical sequence.

2. If the section contains exposition of some classic author, try to read a little of the original. (Suitable editions are listed in the bibliography at the end of the book). You will find that some of the original sources are written in rather difficult language. See if you can pick out of the sources themselves the passages and phrases that are summarized in this book. Always ask this critical question, 'Is this what Plato (or Mill or Kant) is really saying?' Listed at the end of each chapter are commentaries that will help you to do this. Some of these are long. You should use them selectively to seek a better understanding of the particular point or passage that concerns you.

3. When you think you have understood the original authors and followed the complexity of the arguments properly, and once you have set them down as simply and accurately as you can, ask yourself of each stage in the argument, 'Is this true?' If you find that you are inclined to disagree (as on many occasions you will), ask yourself *why* you disagree, and how the view you prefer is to be defended against the criticisms outlined in the book. It is never enough simply to disagree. But if you can formulate a reasoned response, and follow it through in a connected sequence, you will at last have begun to do philosophy. This is the point at which you should turn to the books listed under "Contemporary Discussion". These are books written not for students but for philosophers. In reading these you should follow the same procedures. Try to outline the arguments, check the interpretation of other authors, and ask yourself where you disagree and why. Once you have reached this point, you will be fully engaged in philosophical debate.

CHAPTER ONE

EGOISM: GETTING WHAT YOU WANT OUT OF LIFE

PHILOSOPHY AND THE GOOD LIFE

Most people who come to philosophy for the first time know rather little about it. Nonetheless, they often have a preconceived idea that philosophy ought to raise and answer fundamental questions about how to live, about what things are good and evil, and about the 'meaning' of human life. But the philosophy books they read at the start of their studies frequently seem to have little direct bearing on these topics, and they conclude that their preconceptions about philosophy were mistaken. Sometimes the result is that the newcomers discover an interest in 'academic' philosophy and leave more popular concerns behind. But sometimes they abandon philosophy with a feeling of disappointment.

Either result is regrettable and unnecessary. Though it is indeed wrong to think that philosophers are solely, or even primarily, concerned with the questions philosophy is popularly supposed to address, the popular conception of philosophy is not wholly mistaken. From earliest times, philosophers have tried to stand back from the detailed questions about thought and action that arise in day-to-day living, and to ask what in general a good life for a human being consists in, what makes it good, and whether its being so has any cosmic significance. As we shall see, to raise these questions is to be involved very speedily with the perennial topics of academic philosophy, and it is easy to forget the concerns that began this involvement. Nevertheless, it is the concerns of 'popular' philosophy that provide the context from which the importance of many of the less exciting arguments commonly found in books and journals is derived.

In this book an attempt will be made both to introduce some of the thinkers and arguments that make up the history of academic moral philosophy, and at the same time to keep in view the fundamental questions about how we ought to live and whether our lives have any ultimate meaning. In short, the purpose of this book is to ask what a good life is and to show how philosophy tries to formulate an answer.

INSTRUMENTAL AND INTRINSIC VALUE

To the general question 'What is the most desirable life for a human being?' there is a familiar, if somewhat trite, answer, namely, to be rich and famous. This is a conception of the good life with which those who have not thought much about the question may well concur. Nevertheless, as an answer to the philosopher's question, it does not take us very far. Consider first the aspiration to be rich. If being rich just means having a lot of money, the belief that it is good to be rich turns out to be quite inadequate as an answer to the question with which we started. This is because, strange though it may sound, money in itself has no value whatever. If it were not exchange-able for other, quite different things—goods and services that are independently valuable in their own right—we might as well throw it away.

So accustomed are we to thinking of the notes and coins in our pockets and purses as valuable that the essentially val-ueless character of money is sometimes hard to grasp. But we only have to remind ourselves how worthless foreign currency is once we have returned home to see that it really is so. The only thing that lends money value is its use as a medium of exchange for goods and services which *are* valuable, in themselves.

One way of expressing this feature of money, and which

shows it to be a feature that money shares with many other things, is to say that money has instrumental but not intrinsic value. That is to say, it is valuable only as a way of obtaining something else; it has no value in itself. That this is so becomes evident on those occasions when money cannot be used to obtain anything else. The case of returning home with foreign currency we cannot spend is one obvious example, but more telling in its way is the case of having lots of money in our possession, but finding nothing worth spending it on. Perhaps we find ourselves in a desert with a great deal of money, in need of food and water but with nowhere to buy them.

What this shows is that money is only as valuable as the things it is a means to obtaining. To say that the best life is one in which we are rich, where this means having lots of money, is not really an answer to the question 'What is the best life for a human being?' It does not tell us what to spend our money on.

A related, though somewhat different, point can be made about fame. If being famous is understood merely as being well known to a lot of people, it, too, leaves unanswered the basic question. It does not tell us what we ought to want to be famous for. Is it equally good whether we are famous for life-saving inventions, or for having tortured more children than anyone else in history, or for being the only person to have sung the dwarves' song from *Snow White* for forty-eight hours without stopping? Since we can be famous for quite different kinds of things, some good, some evil, some trivial, some momentous, to be told that it is valuable to be famous is to be told nothing useful until we are told what to be famous *for*.

We might be tempted to suppose that those who want fame and extol its value do not want to be famous for anything in particular, but just to be famous. In one sense this is true, but we can see that fame by itself is not enough. We can easily imagine someone who sets himself to accomplish many things with a view to becoming famous. But let us suppose that his every endeavour meets with spectacular failure. In fact, so extraordinary is his unfailing ability to 'snatch defeat out of the jaws of victory' that he becomes famous as the world's greatest failure. In this roundabout way he has, curiously, accomplished his aim. But we can see that, whatever it was he was aiming at, it would have been more desirable to him to have won fame through success rather than through failure. From this it follows that, whatever our aims, there are better and less good ways of becoming famous. This shows that to the question 'What should we aim at in this life?' the answer 'fame' by itself is insufficient. We need to be told in which way it is best to become famous.

The example of the spectacular failure may suggest an answer. The disappointment he suffered, despite the fame he achieved, arose from the fact that he did not achieve fame in the way he wanted. This seems to imply that what we need to add to the abstract talk of fame is some reference to individual desires. A similar conclusion emerges from the points made above about money. There we saw that money has value only as an instrument, a way of getting something else. This means that in being told to seek riches we are not being told all we need to know, since we also need to know what to spend our riches on. Put like this, an answer seems plain—money is valuable because it enables you to get whatever you want. We might, then, amplify the original suggestion in this way: the best life is one in which you are rich enough to do whatever you want and famous for achieving it.

Even this formulation is not altogether satisfactory, however. What gives riches and fame their value is their connection with helping you to get what you want. If getting what you want is the essence of the good life, there is no reason to make special mention of riches or fame. Most people do want things that require quite a lot of money and many want to engage in activities that attract fame. Even those who do not have expensive tastes will require something in the way of wealth to lead the sort of life they do want. 'Riches' is a relative term, and everyone who wants anything needs to be rich to some degree. But the truth of this shows that riches are not *independently* desirable. The position is not quite the same with fame, but those have no interest in achieving things that impress large numbers of people may still have a good life according to this line of thinking. They don't want fame, but they may still be successful in getting the sort of life they *do* want. It seems then that if we regard the good life as getting what you want, we need not make special mention of either of the things with which we started, namely fame and riches.

SUBJECTIVE AND OBJECTIVE VALUE

The idea that the good life is getting what you want, whatever that may be, has an ancient history in philosophy. In fact, it makes an appearance in dialogues written by the Greek philosopher Plato over two and a half thousand years ago. In many of these dialogues the philosopher is represented by Socrates (who was Plato's teacher). The dialogue takes place between Socrates and various other Greek citizens, as he asks the sorts of question we are concerned with here, namely, just what things are good. Often Plato makes the dialogue a lifelike argument between competing points of view. This is especially marked in two dialogues, the *Gorgias*, where Socrates argues at length with (amongst others) a character called Callicles, and the *Republic*, in the earlier part of which Socrates crosses swords with a character called Thrasymachus. In response to Socrates' efforts to discover what things really are valuable, both Callicles and Thrasymachus take the same sort of line. They argue that it is the desires of individuals which make things valuable, and that the good life, consequently, consists in being successful at getting what you want. If this requires the domination of others and the suppression of their aims in pursuit of your own, so be it. I lead the best life when I get what I want, regardless of how this affects others.

In translations of the *Republic*, this thesis is sometimes rendered: Justice is what is in the interests of the stronger. This is not an illuminating translation nowadays, but the basic idea is clear. Socrates, in both dialogues, argues that knowing what the good life is is something that we discover through our ability to reason, whereas Thrasymachus and Callicles both contend that there is nothing to discover. Rather, faced with the different opportunities presented to us, we must decide what we want and use reasoning to set about getting it. The difference between the two may be expressed in this way. Socrates believes that at least some things are *objectively* valuable, whether or not we want them and regardless of how we feel about them, whereas Callicles and Thrasymachus believe that it is only the individual's subjective desire for something that makes it valuable to him or her, which is to say that the goods of this world are only *subjectively* valuable.

This is, arguably, the longest running intellectual dispute in the history of the world. We find it articulated with great subtlety by Plato two and a half millennia ago, and we can just as easily find it being argued about amongst contemporary philosophers. Over the centuries, however, different versions of the dispute have been distinguished. Indeed, it is arguable that progress in this area of philosophy has consisted chiefly in discovering that there are really several, perhaps related, disputes here. One is a metaphysical debate about the *reality* of value in the abstract. Metaphysicians do not discuss whether we ought to value this or that, pleasure or honesty say, but whether there are such things as values in general. In this way the dispute between objectivity and subjectivity becomes a question of existence—in what sense if any does 'good' exist? Is it in some way 'out there in the world', or is it merely a product of the way human beings regard what is out there? If we describe a picture or a sculpture in terms of its beauty, for instance, are we drawing attention to a descriptive property that it actually has, like being square or six feet tall, or is beauty something only in the eye of the beholder?

Another philosophical dispute is about the analysis of language—when I say that something is good, am I saying anything more than that I like it or approve of it? This is the version of the dispute made famous by the Scottish eighteenth-century philosopher David Hume. Hume thought that he had found an argument that would subvert all of the most familiar schools of philosophy and divinity, an argument that purported to show that, despite the fact that moral utterances take the grammatical form of statements ('That is a very bad thing to do'), they, and evaluative utterances in general, really express the speaker's feelings about things ('I strongly disapprove of that').

Both the metaphysical and the linguistic dimensions of the dispute between subjectivists and objectivists have occupied philosophers for centuries and continue to do so. The quarrel between Socrates and Callicles takes a third form. It is a dispute in moral philosophy, that is, a dispute about the value of different ways of living. Instead of asking, in general, whether there is such a thing as value, or what evaluative utterances mean, we can ask of any proposed value—pleasure, happiness, knowledge, freedom, religious devotion, and so on—whether these things really are valuable. Such questions form the topics of Plato's earlier dialogues. In the later dialogues, as Plato developed philosophical interests of his own and was less tied to the issues and methods that he took over from his teacher Socrates, he became more interested in metaphysics and less in moral philosophy. In fact, the different versions of this great debate tend to become intertwined and, as we shall see, the dispute between Socrates and Callicles makes a very good starting point.

SOCRATES VERSUS THE SOPHISTS

The characters of both Thrasymachus and Callicles are used by Plato to represent the ancient Greek school of philosophers known as the Sophists. In keeping with the general doctrines of this school, Callicles argues that the really admirable people are those who see what they want, work out how to get it, and are neither cowed nor constrained by scruples about what the rest of the world approves or disapproves of. In fact, he construes Socrates' talk of goodness in the abstract as a fancy way of trying to support a certain kind of feebleness on the part of the general run of mankind. Weak-willed and small-minded people, he thinks, *say* that there is 'right' and 'wrong' in human conduct only in order to protect themselves collectively from the actions of those who have the self-confidence and strength of purpose to make the world bend to *their* will. Having this confidence and strength of will, they have neither need nor reason to worry about scruples whose purpose is to provide the weak with a defence against them.

In reply, Socrates adopts a method of argument that philosophers have employed ever since. He takes Callicles' generalized portrait of the admirable man and imagines cases that fit the portrait but that do not seem very admirable. For example, we can imagine someone whose sole ambition is to scratch and who pursues this ambition quite regardless of the view of others about, say, scratching in public. It is true of this individual that he has the independence of mind and the strength of will to pursue his own desires independently of the conventional beliefs of others. At the same time, he appears to live a very impoverished life without anything in it that would call forth our admiration.

Callicles chastises Socrates for reducing the discussion to such a base level, and retorts that the sorts of people he has in mind are the great rulers and conquerors whose will is law and who build vast empires and accomplish mighty deeds through their clear-sighted vision of what it is they want and their force of personality. To reply in this way, however, is to make an important concession, because the man with the miserable ambition whom Socrates invites us to imagine does indeed fit the general principle Callicles advances.

The fact that Callicles draws back in the face of this counterexample allows Plato, through the character of Socrates, to draw an important implication. It is only the character of the things the beggar and the conqueror want and choose to which

Callicles could appeal to defend his preference for the latter and his rejection of the former. But this shows that a good life *cannot* be characterized solely in terms of getting what you want, since in part its goodness depends upon what it is you want. If you want bad or base things, your life will be bad or base. This is enough to show that Callicles must be operating with some conception of *objective* value, since the satisfaction of subjective desire is not enough to explain his preference between the different lives Socrates imagines for him.

At this point in the *Gorgias*, the dialogue moves off in different directions. But there are aspects of the dispute between Socrates and Callicles that are worth pursuing further. Socrates wrings a concession from Callicles by getting him to agree that some lives may consist in getting what you want but may still have nothing good or admirable about them. But what if Callicles had been true to his principle and insisted that, whatever we may think of them, all such lives are indeed equally good, since they are all cases of getting what you want? If so, he would not have been vulnerable to the further argument about objective value, or at least not open to it in the way that Plato develops it. But this does not mean that he would have won the argument. After all, the assertion that the best sort of life is one in which you get what you want, though it may have some initial plausibility, is only an assertion. We have been given no reason to accept it. Callicles never does give us a reason, but it is here that other philosophers have taken up the argument.

PSYCHOLOGICAL EGOISM

The idea that the best life is one in which *I* succeed in getting what *I* want is sometimes called *egoism* (from the Latin *ego* for I). Egoism ought not to be confused with selfishness, which we may describe as the tendency to seek and promote my own benefit above that of others. Egoism merely says that I should try to get what I want out of life. Since it says nothing about *what* I should want, I am free to subscribe to the egoist ideal and at the same time to want things for others. So, for instance, an Albert Schweitzer or a Mother Teresa *could* be an egoist; they live the lives they do because it is what they want to do. But what they want is not to promote their own well-being first and foremost (which would be selfishness) but to promote the well-being of others.

The distinction between egoism and selfishness is not always easy to grasp. It may be made clearer by recalling an episode from the life of the English seventeenth-century philosopher Thomas Hobbes. Hobbes's philosophy was notorious in his day as the philosophy of an egoist and an atheist. On one occasion a clergyman saw him giving money to a beggar and thought this inconsistent with Hobbes's professed view. Surely, he asked, the only reason we have to give to beggars is Christ's commandment to relieve the poor. But Hobbes replied that he gave to the beggar both to relieve the beggar's distress and to relieve his own distress at the sight of the beggar. In other words what moved Hobbes to action was *his own* sense of pity. This made him an egoist, but the fact that he had pity for others shows him not to be selfish. A selfish person is someone who is not moved by the plight of others, who is caused no distress by the distress of others; an egoist is someone who insists that it is his own pity, and not the condition of the poor, which provides a reason for acting.

Once we make the distinction between egoism and selfishness, we can begin to see the outline of an argument that might be used in egoism's favour. If 'getting what you want out of life' is an ideal that carries with it no implication whatever about what it is right or wrong to want (and thus may include highly altruistic wants such as the desire to work for the greater benefit of others), then how could we *not* subscribe to it? To be sure, from the point of view of determining actual behaviour, it is uninformative, because it leaves so many detailed questions unsettled. But since we *can* only pursue those things we want to, we must therefore accept that 'getting what one want's out of life' is a principle to which everyone, automatically, subscribes. At least, so it might be thought. But is it true? Can we strive only for those things *we* want? If so, it certainly follows that getting what we want is, necessarily, a fundamental part of a good life.

The thesis that people only do, and can only do, what they want is usually called *psychological* egoism, because it makes egoistic desire the most fundamental psychological explanation. That is to say, it says that all human actions must, ultimately, be explained in terms of the desires of the people whose actions they are. But on the face of it psychological egoism appears to be false. Surely there are countless examples of people doing something other than what they want? These range from simple domestic examples—I continue to make polite conversation with guests when what I really want to do is go to bed with a good book—to momentous events—the torture victim persists in his silence out of loyalty to his friends when what he would like above all else is for the pain to end. If these are instances of people doing other than they want to, then the claim that people always do what they want is false. It cannot, therefore, be used as an adequate ground for egoism.

In the face of these examples, those who are sympathetic to psychological egoism usually reply that the sorts of instances given are not counterexamples to the thesis at all. There must be some sense, they say, in which I *do* want to be polite, and some sense in which the torturer's victim wants to be loyal to his friends more than he wants the pain to cease, otherwise I would go off to bed and he would answer his tormentor's questions. This reply has two important features. First, it makes a claim about what *must* be the case and not merely what is. What started out as a claim about human psychology—that as a matter of *fact* the actions of human beings are always to be explained as the pursuit of some desire—turns out to be a claim about necessity—the actions *must* flow from desires. Otherwise, the agent in question would never have performed them. But a response of this sort to the counterexamples is unsatisfactory, since it *assumes* the truth of psychological egoism and hence cannot provide a defence of it. Only if psychological egoism is true can we confidently assert that all actions *must* exhibit the wants of the person who performs them. Second, the response shows that psychological egoism is not what we might have thought it was, because it uses 'want' in a special and somewhat idiosyncratic way. This second point needs a rather fuller explanation.

Psychological egoism claims that people only do what they want to do, and that behind every action there must lie a desire to perform it on the part of the person whose action it is. At first this seems to conflict with experiences of our own and in the lives of others where other motives besides that of wanting can be called upon to explain actions. For instance, we normally think that as well as wanting to do something I may do it because it is advantageous, or fashionable or kindly or polite. Or sometimes I do it because I think it is the right thing to do from a moral point of view. And these other motivations can conflict with what I want and may take precedence. If so, what I want does not always explain what I do. Now the egoist's response to this line of thought is to say that each of these other motivations is *a sort of* wanting. I do what is morally right because I want to do what is morally right; I do what is polite because I want to be polite; and so on.

But to analyse other motivations in this way is to alter the normal meaning of 'want' so that it comes to mean not 'have a positive desire for' so much as 'be motivated towards'. Now we can see that the claim of psychological egoism is in fact empty. 'Wanting' here means having some motivation, and it is true by definition that every action must have some motivation behind it, if by 'motivation' we just mean 'whatever it is that explains it'. But this is a far cry from the claim which psychological egoism might have been thought to have been making—that out of all the different kinds of motivation that could lie behind human actions only one, namely 'wanting' in a narrow sense, is ever effectual. This last claim is a substantial and challenging one. On the other hand the counterexamples show it to be false. In responding to the counterexamples in the way described, psychological egoism retreats from this substantial claim about human psychology, to an abstract claim about motivation, one which is true but empty. It relies on using 'want' in a way that is tailor-made to fit the egoist's claims.

ETHICAL EGOISM

It might be thought that in all this argument we have lost sight of the dispute between Callicles and Socrates and the central question about a good life. Psychological egoism was called into play in an attempt to support the claim that the good life consists in getting what you want, whatever that may be, by showing that in fact wants lie at the heart of human motivation. We have now seen that this is true only if we understand 'wants' in a special and quite trivial sense. If we understand it in the more full-blooded sense to mean 'what I would find most pleasing', it appears to be false. People have other reasons for action besides wants of this kind.

But the egoist, especially the egoist of a Calliclean stripe, has another response available at this point. He could abandon the concern with how the human psyche works and assert more baldly that, whatever may be true of human beings as we find them, we *ought* to consider the fulfilling of personal desires as the centrepiece of a good life. This is the doctrine known as *ethical* egoism, which is indeed a doctrine more in keeping with the dispute between Socrates and Callicles, since it is normative. That is to say, it is concerned with what we ought to do and why we ought to do it.

Why ought we to act only on the basis of our own desires? In answering this question, there is a problem about the onus of argument. Upon whom does the burden of proof rest? Does the egoist have to prove to the rest of us that living by our own desires is the best way of living? Or do those who want to reject egoism have to prove that there are better ways of living? Who has to prove what to whom? Unless we have some idea of how to answer this question, we cannot have an idea about where the argument should begin.

This is a common problem in philosophy. Whereas in the law courts the burden of proof (on the prosecution) is laid down by a legal principle—the presumption of innocence— there is in philosophy no easy general way of settling it. In the particular case of egoism, egoists have often thought that it is clear where the burden of proof lies. Since they appeal solely to the individual's own desires and nothing more, and since everyone has some reason to pursue his or her own desires just because they are his or her *own*, those who want to appeal to other considerations (whom we will call moralists) must explain why we should pay any heed to these other considerations.

To put the same point another way, ethical egoists bid me do whatever I want. Since *ex hypothesi* (by the very nature of the case) I already want to do it, there is no logical space, so to speak, to ask what reason I have to do it. But moralists, who appeal to considerations other than my personal desires, must explain what reason I have to override those desires. For example, suppose I am on my way to the theatre because I want to see the play that is on the bill. Should I come across an accident, a moralist might claim that I ought to stop and assist, and so perhaps I ought. But the reasonings advanced in favour of doing so or not doing so are not on a par. Since I already want to go to the theatre, I do not need reasons for continuing in that intention. I need reasons for *not* doing so, and this shows that the burden of proof is on the moralist.

Of course, this is not to imply that there need be any difficulty in meeting it, any more than the presumption of innocence means that it is always difficult to prove people guilty. Some court cases are, as we say, open and shut. Neither does this claim about the burden of proof imply that reasons of the right sort, moral reasons, cannot be given. Most of us will agree that in the imagined case it is easy to find the right sort of reason to persuade me that my intention of going to the theatre must be set to one side because something far more important has cropped up. This is compatible with the view that the burden of proof falls on the moral arguments, and this confirms the idea that in general it falls on those who reject ethical egoism rather than those who accept it. By the very nature of the claim it makes, ethical egoism gives us reason to accept it, something that is not true of alternatives to it.

However, though ethical egoism may enjoy this advantage, it also has weaknesses. The first, though not the most important, is that it is repugnant to most minds. The idea that we should give pride of place to getting what we want just because we want it runs counter to a great deal in the Greek, Jewish, and Christian ethical traditions that have shaped so much of our thinking. From a philosophical point of view, this is not an important weakness, because it cannot be turned into a conclusive objection. Someone persuaded of the desirability of egoism as an ethical creed will not be moved by the idea that it is in conflict with other, opposing, creeds. It is true of any moral view that it runs counter to the views that oppose it. Hence this cannot, by itself be an objection to ethical egoism.

Of course, it *would* be an objection *if* the ethical beliefs of the Judeo-Christian tradition were true. But this is precisely what is brought into question by ethical egoism. If I should love my neighbour as myself, it is not enough to love myself alone. But, of course, what the ethical egoist is looking for is a convincing reason for loving one's neighbour as oneself. And this is all the more necessary because, I have suggested, we don't need an argument for loving ourselves. This is something we necessarily have reason to do.

NIETZSCHE AND THE 'WILL TO POWER'

Conflict with the Judeo-Christian tradition, then, though it may give rise to a poor press, is not an intellectual objection to ethical egoism. Indeed, some philosophers have positively embraced the rejection of Judeo-Christian morality. The most famous of these is undoubtedly the German nineteenth-century writer Friedrich Nietzsche. Nietzsche thought Christian theology was intellectually bankrupt. "The Christian conception of God," he said, "is one of the most corrupt conceptions of God arrived at on earth: perhaps it even represents the low water mark in the descending development of the God type" (*The Anti-Christ*, sect. 18). Nor was he any more sympathetic to the moral implications of Christianity. "Nothing in our unhealthy modernity is more unhealthy than Christian pity" (*The Anti-Christ*, sect. 7). In short, "Christianity has been up to now mankind's greatest misfortune" (sect. 51). Someone who thinks this is unlikely to be impressed by the claim that egoism conflicts with Christian morality. So much the better, he will say. Nietzsche's own philosophy of value is not quite egoistic in the way we have characterized egoism, but a brief examination of it is instructive in this context.

Nietzsche was a professor of Classical Philology at the University of Basel in Switzerland, a post to which he was appointed at the unusually early age of twenty-four. His great reputation, however, has little to do with philology, nor was it made chiefly in academic circles. Indeed, Nietzsche's writings defy any straightforward classification, and he is best thought of simply as a thinker and poet, a 'philosopher' in the more popular sense.

To Nietzsche, the most important fact about the period in which he was living was the destruction of religion at the hands of science. The theory of natural selection developed by Darwin, he thought, had ended forever the possibility of rational belief in God. It was Nietzsche who coined the celebrated slogan "God is dead", and who claimed that " 'Pure spirit' is pure nonsense". But he also held that most people had not registered the enormous significance of the collapse of religion, and in a famous passage from one of his many books he imagines a scene in which the man who thinks that God is dead is regarded by his fellow citizens quite literally as a madman.

If God and the supernatural in general have been irrev-
ocably expelled from human thought, then, in Nietzsche's view,
the whole foundation of traditional values has been removed.
Consequently, everything having to do with values and the
meaning of human existence has to be thought out completely
afresh. The title for a last great book that Nietzsche proposed
but never managed to write was *The Revaluation of All Values*,
the first part of it (which was completed) being called signifi-
cantly *The Anti-Christ*. It was this total restructuring of human
thinking that Nietzsche saw as his special task, a task so enormous that some people suspected him of megalomania, a suspicion confirmed for them by the fact that he did finally go
insane and remained so for the last eleven years of his life. (His
insanity was more likely the result of syphilis than of grandiose
ideas.)

However we regard Nietzsche's intellectual ambitions, the
idea that traditional ways of thinking about good and bad are
exhausted is not so strange. If true, it does leave many questions
waiting for answers. Nietzsche's own attempt to answer those
questions is sustained but neither organized nor systematic. The
most we can do here is consider the general thrust of his thinking. Three ideas are especially important—the will to power,
the 'Übermensch', and eternal recurrence.

Since the question of what human beings *ought to* aspire
to could no longer be answered in traditional religious or mor-
alistic terms, Nietzsche began his rethinking by asking what it
is that *does* move people, and his answer was 'the will to power'.

What is good?—All that heightens the feeling of power, the will to
power, power itself in man.
What is bad?—All that proceeds from weakness.
What is happiness? The feeling that power *increases*—that a resistance
is overcome.
Not contentment, but more power; *not* peace at all, but war; *not*
virtue but proficiency. (*The Anti-Christ*, sect. 2)

It is this answer that makes his philosophy a variety of egoism. By 'the will to power' Nietzsche meant the desire to prevail in the circumstances of struggle that are an essential part of the human condition. (We can see the influence of Darwin at work here.) The will to power is more than just the will to live; it is the will to dominate and overcome the competitive challenges of existence. This conception has been widely misunderstood both by supporters and detractors, but it is easiest to see in what way it ought to be understood if we turn to the second of his three leading ideas, the *Übermensch*.

The German word *Übermensch* is literally translated 'overman', but usually rendered 'superman'. Neither translation is a happy one. The first means nothing in English. The second not only has comic book connotations but arouses ideas of Frankensteinian attempts to engineer physically and intellectually superb human beings. It is this understanding of *Übermensch* that gave rise to the association between Nietzsche's ideas and the Nazis' adulation of the supposedly superior Aryan race. The association was deliberately created by the forerunners of the Nazis (including Nietzsche's sister) and fostered by later Nazi theorists seeking to lend intellectual respectability to their genocidal policies. But it was undoubtedly assisted by Nietzsche's own intemperate language. The passage quoted above, for instance, continues: "The weak and ill-constituted shall perish: first principle of our philanthropy. And one shall help them to do so" (*The Anti-Christ*, sect. 2).

In reality, however, Nietzsche's views have very little to do with Nazism. Indeed, it is worth noting that Nietzsche is repeatedly on record as denouncing both anti-Semitism and German nationalistic fervour. Nietzsche's *Übermensch* is not the tall blond-haired Aryan dreamt of in Nazi mythology but the man in whom the will to power is brought to perfection. (Nietzsche took a view of women that would not be popular today.) He himself gives us the following picture.

. . . a strong, highly cultured human being, skilled in all physical accomplishments, who, keeping himself in check and having reverence for himself, dares to allow himself the whole compass and wealth of naturalness, who is strong enough for this freedom; a man of tolerance, not out of weakness, but out of strength, because he knows how to employ to his advantage what would destroy an average nature; a man to whom nothing is forbidden, except it be a weakness, whether that weakness be called vice or virtue. (*Twilight of the Gods*, sect. 49)

The *Übermensch* is someone completely self-contained as far as the value and meaning of his life is concerned, someone who determines for himself what the values of his life will be and who has self-mastery over his intellectual and emotional life sufficient to realize those values in his own life. Having abandoned every inclination to look towards the supernatural, such a person asserts his own will and prevails against the pressure of conventional morality and unthinking conformity to social norms. "Value is the highest quantum of power that a man is able to incorporate—a man: not mankind" (*The Will to Power*, p. 886).

Nietzsche's own declared models of 'supermen' were Julius Caesar and the German poet Goethe. He was heavily influenced in his thinking, however, by his acquaintance with the composer Richard Wagner, whom for a time he admired enormously. Though in the end they fell out, in many ways Wagner provides the best illustration of what Nietzsche had in mind when he talked of *Übermensch*. Wagner was a composer of opera on a very grand scale. His famous *Ring* cycle of operas was so large a conception that it was finally performed only when Wagner was able to construct a purposely built theatre of his own at Bayreuth in southern Germany. The idea of opera on this scale sprang from an equally large artistic ambition, namely to set Art on the right path by creating an art form, grand opera, in which all the fine arts—the visual, the musical, and the dramatic—would be united. In advancing this conception, Wagner was not only rejecting a great many of the artistic conventions of the day. He was, in his own eyes at any rate, establishing his own artistic values.

As an individual, Wagner had an enormously dominant personality. He attracted to himself many devoted disciples, and in the pursuit of his ambitions disregarded many social taboos. For a time Nietzsche was one of his most ardent followers. It is hard to say just what the cause of their rupture was. Nietzsche showed too much independence of thought, perhaps, and Wagner became too self-important. Nietzsche's own explanation was that Wagner had eventually succumbed to stifling traditional German ways of thinking. It is not hard to see, however, what there was in Wagner that Nietzsche could ascribe to the *Übermensch*. Here was a man who, by the sheer force of his will, personality, and vision, was able to rise above the artistic values he had inherited and create new values for himself.

In a moment we will look again at Nietzsche's attitude to Wagner for the light it throws on his thought about values. First we must consider the third of his principal ideas, eternal recurrence. Nietzsche was much struck by the thought that the matter in the universe is finite and the number of configurations it can assume is finite, while time is infinite. It follows that any configuration of matter will eventually recur and, since time is infinite, will recur again and again for all eternity. This is the belief in 'eternal recurrence'. If it is true that any configuration of matter will, given time, recur, it is true that we ourselves, being configurations of matter in time, will recur again and again. The perception that this is so gives us a standard by which to judge the actions we perform and the characters we develop. We can ask not merely whether they meet up to the standards of the day, but whether they are fit for eternal recurrence. In this curious way, the Christian conception of life as a preparation for eternity makes a reappearance in the writings of the anti-Christian Nietzsche.

This is a very brief summary of Nietzsche's voluminous

writings and to set them out in this simple way disguises the fact that a great deal of what he wrote was more poetry than philosophy, aphorism rather than argument, and that his books contain many conflicts and contradictions. Nevertheless, enough has been said to allow us to examine the fundamentals of his thought. Nietzsche saw supreme value in the individual's 'will to power'. The basis of this belief was his conviction that the foundation of traditional values—religion—had been destroyed. In a sense, nothing could replace it, but the *Übermensch* rises above this calamity by recognizing it, accepting it and creating value and meaning for himself through his own 'will to power'. We will have to examine the idea of individual creation of value more closely when we come to the discussion of existentialist writers in Chapter Three. Here it is important to note that clearly what impressed Nietzsche was the idea of a solitary individual making sense of fundamental chaos and uncertainty by relying on nothing other than his own will and strength of purpose. It is for this reason that his thinking may be said to be egoistic.

Yet it is never clear just why the exercise of the will to power is to be valued, and hence it remains unclear what mode of human existence best exemplifies it. There is much talk of *'life'* (usually italicized) and 'strength' and 'power'. These are all spoken of as what we might call heroic values. The trouble is that they all appear to be valuable *instrumentally*, not intrinsically. They leave us asking, 'The value of *life* for what?' 'The value of strength and power to do what?' Some of the things he says suggest that Nietzsche would deny that 'the will to power' is of purely instrumental value. It is the will to power for its own sake that is to be valued. But why should we value the will to power if it expresses itself in meanness or triviality? Nietzsche himself loathed and despised many of the attitudes of the Germans of his generation, but nothing that he says prevents these despicable attitudes from being themselves expressions of the will to power.

To see the force of this point, we should consider the case

of Wagner once more. Nietzsche for a time admired Wagner enormously because of the great force of his personality and his apparent disregard for those German values that Nietzsche thought small-minded. But after some years he came to think that Wagner succumbed to those very values he had earlier transcended. In short, he became a typical German of the sort Nietzsche greatly despised. There is reason to think that Nietzsche's view of Wagner was heavily influenced by personal factors. But whatever the historical truth, it is easy to see that this change on Wagner's part need not in itself give Nietzsche any reason to change his assessment. This is because, even if it is true that Wagner's work came to embody values he had hitherto disregarded (German patriotic fervour expressed in mythology and so on), it could still be true that he did this in the clear knowledge of the historical crisis of which Nietzsche made so much, and by virtue of his own will and personality. In short, whatever values Wagner's work represented could be a result of 'life', an exercise of 'strength' and 'the will to power'. It is the *heroic* character of Wagner's personality and way of life that impressed Nietzsche, but the trouble is that the 'will to power' need result in nothing heroic and can light upon those very things that Nietzsche loathed.

Of course, it might be said that this leaves out of the picture the idea of eternal recurrence. Not every expression of the will to power is fit for all eternity. Why not? Whatever the answer to this question, it must be found, not in references to the will to power, but to the sorts of things that will results in. The idea of fitness for eternal recurrence seems intended to apply to people like Julius Caesar, whose life stands as an example of great generalship across the centuries, but it can as easily be applied to examples of great indolence or fraud. Nietzsche says that the *Übermensch* is "a man to whom nothing is forbidden, except it be a weakness." But he himself *wants* to forbid some things—endorsement of bourgeois German piety, for instance. What he does not see, however, is that these things need not arise from weakness, but could arise from *life* and strength. Nietzsche's philosophy of value suffers from precisely the same fault as Callicles' more straightforward egoism. It can only give an account of subjective value but requires some account of objective value as well.

THE OBJECTIVE VALUE OF ETHICAL EGOISM: WHY SHOULD I DO WHAT I WANT?

By pursuing Nietzsche's philosophy this far, we have in fact returned to the dispute between Socrates and Callicles. We saw that Socrates was able to refute Callicles by wresting from him an agreement that some ways of getting what you want are not admirable, because of the kinds of wants they are. So, if we take the touchstone and the sole criterion of the admirable life to be getting what you want, the drunkard whose ambition is to lie drunk among the garbage of the city as much as possible can be said to live as admirable a life as that of a ruler, through whose strength of will and visionary purpose law and order are brought to a vast empire. Callicles, of course, was highly reluctant to make this comparison, and for that reason was forced to abandon the egoistic principle on which he had built his argument.

In a similar fashion we have seen that those who espouse ethical egoism, or who view human will as central to the creation of value in the way Nietzsche does, can be forced into conceding that what matters is not just the assertion of will and desire but the assertion of *heroic* will and desire. This amounts to a concession that ethical egoism—we ought to strive for what we want—is an inadequate answer to the question 'How ought we to live?' But the argument has also advanced a little. The discussion of ethical egoism has not left us in the same position as the discussion of the dispute between Callicles and Socrates. There Socrates appeals to a counterexample. Its force depends upon our accepting (as Callicles does) that the life described, though it fits the principle, is not admirable. Of course, we are free to reject or just to question this judgement. Is the life of the happy beggar really any worse than the life of a happy prince? The beggar does not have all that the prince does, but does this matter if he doesn't want it? As a consequence, the argument against Callicles is necessarily inconclusive.

The argument we have just considered against ethical egoism, on the other hand, is not quite the same as that against Callicles. If we hold, not that people are so constituted they will only do what they want (psychological egoism) but rather that one *ought* to strive for what one desires, then we must regard those who do not follow their heart's desires as making a mistake, and regard this as still a mistake *whatever their state of mind*. Thus, faced with a group of people who, after the fashion of Buddhist monks, make every effort to suppress and conquer their fleshly desires, and who are so successful that they come to be without anything we commonly call desires, the proponents of ethical egoism are bound to say that theirs is, *objectively* speaking, less good than another, more self-centered, human life.

This implication follows from the fact that ethical egoism is a *doctrine*. It recommends the pursuit of personal desire over other sorts of life and must therefore rule out a life of self-denial, even if those who deny themselves come to like the life they lead. It might be replied that the Buddhist monks are not evidence against the egoistic ideal. Though they alter their desires, they still end up doing what they want. To reply in this way, however, provides only a temporary respite. A Buddhist monk might say that the question is 'What should I want, if I am to find the path to peace and happiness?' It is dogmatism for egoists to argue that getting whatever I want must make me happy. Many people have hurtful or even self-destructive desires (drug addicts, for instance). But if getting what I want does not necessarily lead to happiness, why should I adopt the egoistic principle as the basis of my life and conduct? At the very least I need to be told what wants are good for me.

From this two important further consequences follow. First, contrary to initial appearances, ethical egoism does suppose that there is objective right and wrong in the way people choose to live. A life lived according to what the eighteenth-century Scottish philosopher David Hume called "the monkish virtues" must be plainly wrong according to the ethical egoist, if, that is to say, ethical egoism is to have any substance as a doctrine about how we ought to live. Second, there is a deficiency in the principle as stated so far. We can intelligibly ask what things it is best for us to want, and the assertion 'The good life consists in getting what you want' cannot supply any answer.

DESIRES AND INTERESTS

One response to this and to other objections says that philosophical egoism has been misrepresented. The most plausible version of egoism is not about desires but about *interests*. The difference between desires and interests is this. My desires are those things I experience as longings or inclinations. My interests are those things which are of vital importance to my life and well-being. Something is in my interest if it promotes that well-being. But what is in my interest need not always coincide with what I want or desire at any given moment. For instance, even though I am asthmatic I may want to smoke but recognize that it is not in my interest to do so. Or I may have a strong desire to spend the morning in bed but recognize that to do so would be to forfeit my job and would thus be contrary to my interest. If I am an egoist about my interests, I have on occasion good reason to combat my desires.

There is thus an alternative version of egoism to that we have been considering. It says not that you should pursue your own desires, but rather always promote your own interests. The best life, on this conception, is not one in which you succeed in getting what you want whenever you want it, but in which you succeed in getting what is in your interests over the long term. This revised form of egoism has two advantages over the simple desire version. To begin with, it supplies the basis of a reply to the sorts of counterexample we have considered. We can now say that is not in the interests of the drunk or the drug addict to give into immediate desires. Consequently, egoism is not committed to commending these modes of life. In the second place, we can acknowledge without difficulty that this sort of egoism employs the idea of objective value. Some things are as a matter of fact in my interests, and other things are not. I can be mistaken about these and desire all the wrong things. So to the question 'What ought I to want?' egoism *does* have an answer; you ought to want what is in your interests. If anyone were to raise the further question 'Why should I do what is in my interests?' the egoist can reply 'Because it is in your interests' and insist that there is nothing more to be said.

This line of argument is a very plausible one, and many philosophers have supposed that it does supply all we need for thinking about every aspect of values. It may *seem* to omit the claims of altruism, that is to say, doing what is in the interests of others in preference to what is in our own interests. But many philosophers, following Thomas Hobbes, have argued that it does not do so. This is because in real life it is in our own best interests as individuals to be altruistic and to observe common moral duties and obligations. In this way, they think, rational egoism provides the best basis for morality one could hope for.

It is a line of thought we will return to in future chapters. For the moment, let us concede the following points: Egoism that refers to interests rather than desires can cope with simple counterexamples. It provides a conception of objective value, while at the same time explaining its rational appeal. And it is a foundation upon which duties to others besides ourselves may be built. However, there remains an important question: What *is* in my interests?

Arguably, the fact that this question remains unanswered means that all the important questions about the good life remain to be settled. We can see this by observing that Socrates could agree with the revised version of egoism. His claim is that it is in my interests to lead the best possible life. His dispute with Callicles and Thrasymachus is about what this life consists in. Here another strand of thought in the dialogues comes into play. It is implicit in what many people, including Callicles, say that they mean by 'in my interest', those things I find most pleasing or gratifying. Thus egoism becomes confused (or at least intertwined) with the view that gratification and pleasure (and the avoidance of pain) are what constitute a good life. But this is in fact a distinct philosophy of value, known as 'hedonism' from the Greek word for pleasure. It is a view well worth exploring, but it requires a chapter to itself.

SUGGESTED FURTHER READING

Original Sources
Plato, *The Republic*, book 1, and *The Gorgias*
Nietzsche, *Twilight of the Gods* and *The Anti-Christ*

Commentaries
Terence Irwin, *Plato's Moral Theory*
R J Hollingdale, *Nietzsche: The Man and His Philosophy*

Contemporary Discussions
Thomas Nagel, *The Possibility of Altruism*
David Gautier, *Morals by Agreement*

CHAPTER TWO

HEDONISM: PLEASURE AND HAPPINESS

In the last chapter we saw that egoism, defined as getting what you want, is not an adequate conception of the best sort of life for a human being. Its strength is supposed to be that it locates the motive for the good life in subjective desire and not in any abstract conception of 'the good', but try as we might, we cannot avoid questions about the relative value of the various desires that human beings have. In other words, we cannot avoid asking what we ought to want, and it is this question that a desire-based egoism fails to answer.

In order to overcome this and other difficulties, we considered a redefinition of egoism in terms of interests—the good life is one in which you successfully promote your own interests. This version does tell us what we ought to want—we ought to want what is in our own best interests. But as any one can see, this answer does not take us much further forward. We now need to know what is in our best interests; what are the best things to want? In the history of philosophy, an answer to this question is provided by a doctrine closely associated with the egoism we have just discussed. This is hedonism—the belief that the best life is that which is most pleasurable. So close is the association between egoism and hedonism that it is not always easy to distinguish the two views. In the *Gorgias*, for instance, the dialogue discussed in the last chapter, the views Callicles espouses are both egoistic and hedonistic.

THE CYRENAICS

In fact, however, the ancient school of philosophy that first espoused the philosophy of hedonism was not the Sophists (the label usually given to Gorgias and Callicles) but the Cyrenaics, named after the birthplace of their founder Aristippus of Cyrene, a Greek town in what is now Libya. The Cyrenaics held that pleasure is the only natural good there is. That is to say, pleasure, and pleasure only, is universally recognized by all human beings to be desirable. Conversely, pain is a natural evil, something acknowledged the world over as undesirable. Consequently, to commend as the best life one that has as much pleasure and as little pain as possible in it is to speak in terms that human beings of all cultures and periods can appreciate. This is the force of saying that pleasure is a natural good and pain a natural evil.

In this, pleasure and pain differ markedly from such things as honour and disgrace. The difference has two aspects. In the first place, honour is not universally regarded as something good or disgrace as something bad. In some cultures, people have a very strong sense of family honour, for instance, and regard with horror anything that sullies the family name. In other cultures, people have no such sense. In the second place, just what counts as honourable and which things are to be regarded as disgraceful are matters that differ from culture to culture. Whereas the things that cause pain cause it anywhere, the things that cause disgrace in one context may be quite without significance in another. For example, in any society it is an evil to develop a cancerous growth. For an unmarried woman to become pregnant is a disgrace only in some societies. One effect of this is that, unlike pleasure and pain, ideals based upon the pursuit of honour and avoidance of disgrace often disintegrate in the face of quite different and competing conceptions of what life should be like. We can deliberately reject the idea that unmarried pregnancies are disgraceful, whereas we cannot reject the fact that cancerous growths are painful. Another effect is that honour and disgrace are values highly dependent upon the customs and practices of particular times and places. The honour to which a mediaeval knight aspired can hardly be an aspiration for us. We can, of course, dress up and compete on horseback in the same way, but what was a real way of life for them can only be a game for us because the social world in which we live has changed. By contrast, the natural world does not change.

In these two ways, pain and pleasure differ from other values. This is what is meant by calling them 'naturally' good and evil, a feature which puts hedonism at a decided advantage over other possible philosophies of value. Or so the Cyrenaics and others have thought. It is a question to which we will return, but first there are other problems to be raised. If we accept for the moment that pleasure is the only natural good and that this gives us reason to make the pursuit of pleasure and the avoidance of pain our main aim in life, we are still faced with the question 'What mode of life will supply the greatest amount of pleasure?' According to the Cyrenaics, who held the popular version of hedonism, the best life is one as full as possible of bodily pleasures—food, drink, sex, and the like. This vision of the good life still has its devotees. But if we were to take it seriously, we should soon discover that though pleasure and pains are opposites—the one good, the other evil—in the most straightforward contexts they commonly *accompany* each other. The result is that in the pursuit of bodily pleasure it is virtually impossible to avoid bodily pains.

For example, the pleasure of a good meal is in part dependent upon appetite, which is to say hunger. It is only by suffering (at least to a small degree) the pangs of hunger that we can really take pleasure in the feast that follows. Similarly, it can be enormously pleasurable to get wildly drunk, but this will usually be followed by intense nausea and headaches. Or again, the injection of heroin is said by those who know about these things to induce a bodily and mental sensation of unsurpassed pleasure. But it also numbs the senses so that those under its influence often injure themselves and suffer considerable pain and discomfort later on. Nor is the pleasure of sex unalloyed. Some people (perhaps all of us at some moments) find what is commonly regarded as illicit sex alluring. But to engage in it, in the world as it is, would be to run the risk of VD, herpes, AIDS, and other painful, sometimes fatal, ailments. Even relatively safer forms of sexual gratification—pornographic shows and movies, for instance—usually bring some downside with them, if only the exorbitant price of compulsory drinks and the tawdry accommodation in which they are customarily offered.

The Cyrenaics' ideal of the good life, therefore, is more attractive in theory than it is likely to be in real life. If we take it seriously, we shall see that it is unrealizable and hence worthless as an ideal. This is a point worth stressing. Those who do not take easily to the injunctions of moralizers or the religious 'joy' of the pious often have the sneaking suspicion that, if it were not for the constraints of upbringing and convention, we would all agree that a life of pleasure of the most straightforward kind cannot be beaten. But in fact, as we have seen, it is far from clear that such a life would indeed be possible, regardless of social convention and constraint. There are many clear examples of this. One is gluttony. This is no longer regarded as a sin, but those who indulge too much in the pleasure of eating become obese and subject to all the ailments and diseases obesity commonly brings. Another is cigarette smoking. Most people smoke for the pleasure it gives, but again excess not infrequently leads to painful, sometimes incurable, diseases of the heart and lungs. Occasionally those who suffer life-threatening illness as a result of smoking or overeating think that the pleasure they have had more than compensates even for such a dreadful end. Still, this does not alter the point that the pursuit of a life filled with pleasure and devoid of pain proved, in these cases, impossible.

THE EPICUREANS

This impossibility, however, is not a logical one but a contingent one. There is no necessary connection between drunkenness and hangovers or homosexual promiscuity and AIDS. These pleasures bring pains just because of the way the world happens to be. What this implies is that the flaw in the Cyrenaics' conception of the good life is not that it gives pride of place to pleasure, but that it gives pride of place to some *kinds* of pleasure, namely straightforward bodily ones. This is a point observed by, amongst others, the ancient Greek philosopher Epicurus, who gave his name to an alternative version of hedonism, namely, Epicureanism. (From what we know of Epicurus, this is something of a misnomer, since his philosophical interests were chiefly concerned with quite different questions.)

This Epicurean version of hedonism is to be found reflected in common speech. An 'epicure' is someone who savours the finer things of life—good wine, good food, good company, urbane literature, elegant dress, and so on—and this use of the word faithfully reflects the view of the Epicureans that if life is to be filled with pleasure it can only be filled with those pleasures that, generally, do not have accompanying pains. And these, we should observe, will be relatively mild and gentle pleasures—good wine but not too much of it, delicately flavoured light meals of the sort that will appeal to the gourmet but not upset the digestive system, music and drama that delight but do not stir debilitating emotions, and so on. In fact, as this range of examples indicates, the Epicureans' philosophy of pleasure and the good life is to be contrasted quite sharply with popular conceptions of hedonism, since it contains very little that would commonly be described as an indulgence. Indeed, it actually requires its adherents to forswear many of the things that people generally find most pleasurable.

It does so, of course, because it is only these refined and gentle pleasures that are without accompanying pains and hence only these pleasures that are capable of *filling* a life. But at the same time it is rather evident that these are *acquired* pleasures, the pursuit of which would require a good deal of constraint on the part of those who sought pleasure in this way. We do not naturally restrict ourselves to a glass or two of the best wine. Left to their own devices, more people will take pleasure in the noise and rhythm of rock 'n' roll or heavy metal than will savour the delicate harmonies of Boccherini's *Minuet*. This raises an important question. If Epicureanism advocates a life of pleasure of the sort we must learn to acquire, can it continue to claim the 'natural' appeal which earlier appeared to be hedonism's great advantage over other philosophies? The excesses of the Cyrenaic hedonism are mitigated in the Epicurean version. But if this is at the expense of a foundation in 'natural' pleasures and pains, the gain would appear to be more than outweighed by the loss.

JOHN STUART MILL AND HIGHER AND LOWER PLEASURES

Hedonism is the view that pleasure is a natural good and the only natural good there is, and that pain is, correspondingly, the only natural evil. We have now seen, however, that were we to seek to maximize the pleasure in our lives and minimize the pain, we would end up leading a certain sort of life, an Epicurean one, and a sort of life different to that which hedonism is commonly thought to recommend. Hedonism is, then, a real philosophy of life—it gives us clear guidance about the best way to live. But the style of life it prescribes will not appeal to everyone. Those who aspire to moral endeavour or artistic achievement, say, will find it unworthy, and those who seek passion and excitement will think it dull. This means that it is *not* universally appealing, which is what pleasure is supposed to be. The fact is that the life of pleasure recommends only some pleasures. Whatever may be true of pleasure in the abstract, it is not true that any given set of pleasures, including the set of pleasures hedonism ends up recommending, are in any sense naturally good.

This is shown in part by the fact that we can, apparently, make intelligible discriminations between pleasures. This was a possibility with which a much more recent philosopher was greatly concerned. John Stuart Mill was a nineteenth-century English philosopher. Like the Cyrenaics and the Epicureans, he believed that pleasure was a natural good and pain a natural evil and consequently it is in terms of pleasure and pain that the good life is to be assessed. But he also recognized that there are intelligible distinctions to be made between the lives that people lead which cannot be straightforwardly explained in terms of pleasure. Here is an example that he has made famous: We can imagine a pig whose life is pretty well filled with swinish pleasures and we can imagine a Socrates whose intellectual achievements, though enormous, have resulted in the frustrating perception that his greatest achievement is to appreciate just how little he knows. The pig is satisfied and Socrates dissatisfied, so that hedonism would appear to commend the life of the pig. But Mill thought it obvious (as most of us will probably agree) that the life of a Socrates dissatisfied is better than the life of a pig satisfied. This must lead us to wonder how any appeal to pleasure as the sole thing which is good in itself could explain this difference. In an attempt at explanation, Mill introduced a distinction between higher and lower pleasures. Pleasure is indeed the touchstone of value, he thought, but some pleasures are better than others.

How can this be? Surely, if we declare some pleasures better than others, we must be invoking a standard of 'better' *other than* the standard of pleasure itself. If so, this shows that pleasure is not the only good there is. Two moves are commonly made in an effort to avoid this conclusion. First, it is sometimes said that the difference between higher and lower pleasures is to be explained in terms of *quantity* of pleasure. A higher pleasure brings *more* pleasure. However, such a distinction is entirely superficial. It cannot show any fundamental difference between pleasures because it makes higher and lower pleasures commensurable. That is to say, we can arrive at a pleasure equivalent to the highest of pleasures if only we add enough of the lowest pleasures up. For instance, suppose we take the reading of Shakespeare to be a higher pleasure, and the eating of doughnuts to be a lower one. If the only difference between the two is quantity of pleasure, we can attain the equivalent of a pleasure in great drama if we eat a large enough quantity of doughnuts.

Of course, someone might accept this conclusion and agree that pleasures are commensurable, that the pleasures of Shakespeare or Beethoven *can* be compensated by sufficient numbers of doughnuts or episodes of *Dallas*. But agreeing that this is so is tantamount to denying that there are different kinds of pleasure. From this it follows that quantity of pleasure cannot provide us with the means to discriminate between pleasures in the way that Mill wanted to.

Mill himself, however, did not appeal to quantity but to quality. He thought that higher pleasures brought a different and better *quality* of pleasure. It is difficult to know whether this appeal provides any solution at all. Does the idea of a better quality of pleasure not already invoke a standard of better and worse other than pleasure itself? Even if it does not, the suggestion is unhelpful in another way, because the way Mill explains it we cannot actually tell higher quality pleasures from lower quality ones.

We can see this by exploring the method for discriminating between pleasures that he proposed—namely, asking those who have experience of both higher and lower pleasures which they prefer. On the face of it, this seems a sensible proceeding; who could be a better judge between two things than the person who has experience of both? But in reality this method achieves nothing. Suppose we ask someone who has listened to both opera and country music which is the higher pleasure and his answer is opera. There are two possible explanations of this answer. It *could* be that the two sorts of music generate different qualities of pleasure, that he has the sensitivity to discriminate between them, and that he has found the pleasure opera supplies to be of a higher calibre than that supplied by country and western. On the other hand, it could just as easily be that he simply finds opera more pleasurable because his tastes in music run this way. It is obviously important for those who want to distinguish between higher and lower pleasures that his judgement is explained in the first and not in the second way. Yet how could we ever know that this was so? And if we cannot, we do not have any means of discriminating between quality of pleasures. So we could call upon the testimony of any number of 'judges', but we would not be accumulating evidence in any significant way, since each verdict would be open to this same ambiguity of interpretation.

Nor did Mill (or anyone) ever actually use this method. Indeed, Mill thought he knew which pleasures were higher pleasures in advance of any method, so that if someone who had tried both had actually told him that warm baths were a higher pleasure than philosophy, he would have dismissed this as the judgement of an ignoramus. This suggests that Mill regarded the appeal to the authority of competent judges not as *evidence* of higher pleasures but as a *criterion*. In declaring some pleasure to be of a higher quality, the competent judge does not provide us with evidence. Rather, the pleasure in question is a higher one *just because* competent judges prefer it. So, for instance, we can say that a piece of music gives a higher quality of pleasure, if it is a fact that those who know a great deal about music prefer it, just as we can declare a wine to be of higher quality if it is preferred by those who have done a lot of wine tasting.

There are several problems with this alternative interpretation. Is there in fact sufficient unanimity between competent judges, or would we find that the 'quality' of a pleasure varies depending upon whom we ask? Must competent judges prefer on grounds of pleasure, or are there other grounds upon which their preferences might be based? Even if these questions can be answered satisfactorily, there remains the same question as before. How do we know that those who have listened to a lot of music or done a great deal of wine tasting have *more refined* tastes, and not merely *different* tastes from those who have not? Until this question is answered, Mill's account of higher and lower pleasures, whichever way we interpret it, remains a piece of arbitrary stipulation.

The appeal to higher and lower pleasures, then, accomplishes little and raises more questions than it settles. It is important to stress, however, that nothing that has been said so far runs counter to the view, which Mill obviously shared, that some of the activities in which human beings take pleasure are better than others. All that has been shown is that the mark of their being better cannot be that they are productive of a higher pleasure. We can indeed take pleasure in 'higher' things, but what makes them 'higher' is not the pleasure they give us, but something else about the activities themselves. From this it follows that there must be some other good than pleasure, and hence that strict hedonism is false.

SADISTIC PLEASURES

A hedonist might reply that this refutation of hedonism succeeds only if we first accept one of the premises from which Mill's argument began, namely, that the life of a Socrates dissatisfied is better than that of a pig satisfied. But perhaps we need not accept this. Indeed, a consistent hedonist ought not to. If pleasure is the only natural good, then any life filled with pleasure is as good as any other and better than a life with pain and dissatisfaction. To accept this is to accept that, contrary to what Mill and perhaps most people think, Socrates has reason to envy the pig, since the pig leads a better life. The fact that neither we nor Socrates, given our abilities and interests, would find pleasurable the sort of life the pig likes misleads us into thinking that the pig's life is not a good one. But it is, since it is filled with pleasure, and pleasure is the sole natural good.

Of course, a human life filled with pleasure will contain many activities different to that of the pig, but it will not contain any more *pleasure*, and hence will not be any better. Thus, it can be argued, hedonism avoids the difficulties which Mill's appeal to higher and lower pleasures encounters, by denying that there *are* any differences in the merits of different kinds of pleasures.

Such a denial brings us back, in fact, to the dispute between Socrates and Callicles considered in the last chapter. Socrates, it will be recalled, drew Callicles' attention to the fact that, as far as satisfaction of wants goes, there is no difference between those who succeed in the demanding and ennobling tasks they set themselves, and those who succeed in the lazy and vulgar life-styles with which they are content. The point can as easily be put in terms of pleasure. If pleasure is all that matters, we cannot justify a preference for the pleasure that a surgeon takes in saving the life of a child by means of an immensely demanding operation over the pleasure a sadist takes in the sufferings of the animal he is torturing. Yet it seems obvious to most people that there is a crucially important difference between the two.

This particular example is mine, but Callicles, it will be recalled, when presented by Socrates with a contrast between heroic and vulgar pleasures, accepts that there is indeed a difference to be explained. It is this acceptance which provides the means for his defeat. Had he not accepted this difference, the argument would have had to take a different direction. Similarly, if a thoroughgoing hedonist were to insist that in so far as it is true that a torturer gets just as much pleasure from his trade as does a healer they lead equally good lives, then an appeal to alleged differences between the two cannot provide a counter to his thesis. A consistent hedonist does not have the problem Callicles does.

To some minds, this will show just how depraved a philosophy hedonism is. But to philosophers this is not so evident. In the first place, we should note that the hedonists are not recommending torture as a way of life. Neither is hedonism necessarily egoistic, concerned only with one's own pleasure. Hedonists need not deny that the lives of the torturer's victims are about as bad as can be. On the contrary, given the hedonist view of pain, they are likely to assert this positively. Their view is, rather, that if someone, with a highly abnormal psychology, no doubt, were to enjoy torture in exactly the way that most of us enjoy our favourite activities, then his life would be as enjoyable as ours. This is not to say that the torturer has had a good life. Since he has caused a lot of pain and suffering, there is much, from the hedonist point of view, to be said against it. But there is at least this to be said for it—he has derived pleasure from it.

It is this last point that flies in the face of received wisdom. Whereas hedonism thinks that the sadists' getting pleasure from their hurtful activities counts in their favour, even though it does not shift the overall balance from negative to positive, to most people the same fact makes them *worse*, not better. Still, though such a view may be contrary to conventional wisdom and highly unpalatable to most people, the radical character of their inquiries in other branches of the subject has made philosophers aware that the mere fact that some view or other is unconventional or unpopular does not in itself show it to be false. To refute hedonism as a philosophy of value, something more is needed than an appeal to counterintuitive examples of the sort we have been considering. In order to find a most substantial objection, we should now turn to another Greek philosopher, Aristotle.

ARISTOTLE ON PLEASURE

Aristotle was a student of Plato, for a time tutor to Alexander the Great, and director of the Lyceum at Athens, where he lectured on and conducted original research into almost every branch of human knowledge. Most of his thought has come down to us by means of the notes of his students, and it is in one such set of lecture notes, called the *Nicomachean Ethics*, that his thoughts on pleasure are to be found. Aristotle was not averse to the view that pleasure is a good, or even that it is a principal good. But he thought that we cannot adequately assess the merits of hedonism unless we inquire closely into what is meant by pleasure. When hedonists recommend pleasure, just what are they recommending? We began with an opposition between pleasure and pain. It is in terms of this opposition that the Cyrenaic and Epicurean versions of hedonism are formulated. Yet it is clear that there is an important asymmetry between the two. The word 'pain' can be used to refer both to a particular kind of bodily sensation, and to any unwanted experience in general. A knife can cause a pain in my leg, and an unkind remark can also give me pain. But the two sorts of pain are not the same. The first is a locatable sensation, the other a psychological experience.

When we speak of pleasure, however, we cannot be referring to a locatable sensation. I can have a pain in my leg, but never a pleasure. Of course, some bodily sensations can be *pleasurable*—the sensations associated with food, drink, and sex, for instance—but this does not make pleasure itself a sensation. Food, drink, sex, and so on are productive of pleasurable sensations rather than productive of pleasure. This is an important point to grasp for two reasons. First, it throws a different light on the idea that pleasure is a *natural* good. Let us agree that there is reason to call physical pain a natural evil because it is a sensation that humans and other animals instinctively seek to avoid. (It should be noted that not all philosophers accept that pain is in this sense a natural evil.) But if there is no sensation of pleasure corresponding to that of pain, there is nothing that is a natural good in quite the way that pain is a natural evil. The most we can say is that there are sensations that are pleasurable—those associated with sex for instance—and that people naturally seek these sensations. Whether they seek them *because* they are pleasurable is another matter. Consequently, even if we agree that human beings naturally seek sexual gratification, we cannot straight off conclude that they naturally seek pleasure. At the very least, the picture is more complex than it is with pain.

A second implication of the asymmetry between pain and pleasure is this. While there are indeed pleasurable sensations, other things can be pleasurable also. A warm bath may be pleasurable, but so can a conversation, or a game of tennis. Because they were specially impressed with the pain/pleasure distinction, the early hedonists tended to overlook the fact that other things besides sensations can be pleasurable, and when they spoke of pleasure they focussed upon pleasurable sensations. As Aristotle says:

No one nature or state either is or is thought the best for all, neither do all pursue the same pleasure; yet all pursue pleasure. . . . But the bodily pleasures have appropriated the name both because we oftenest steer our course for them and because all men share in them; thus, because they alone are familiar, men think there are no others. (*Nichomachean Ethics*, book 7, chap. 13)

In other words, pleasure is not one thing. Consequently, though it is true (in Aristotle's view) that human beings seek pleasure, this does not imply that they all seek one type of sensation. In fact,

there are actually pleasures that involve no pain or appetite . . . pleasures [include] activities and ends . . . ; and not all pleasures have an end different from themselves . . . this is why it is not right to say that pleasure is perceptible process. (*Nichomachean Ethics*, book 7, chap. 12)

What Aristotle means to emphasize here is that activities that are engaged in for pleasure may differ in important respects. Someone may engage in sexual intercourse for the pleasurable sensations it produces. In this case, in Aristotle's language, the pleasure resides in the end of the activity, the sensations it produces. But not all pleasurable activities are like sex. Golf, for instance, gives great pleasure to many millions of people, but to play golf for pleasure is not to play for some end independent of the activity itself. The pleasure does not lie in some special sensation that swinging a golf club produces, but in the game itself. This is what he means by saying that "not all pleasures have an end different from themselves."

In short, there are different kinds of pleasure, and it is a mistake to suppose, as crude versions of hedonism do, that looking for pleasure is a matter of seeking the means to induce pleasurable sensations. Sometimes it does, but more often than not it doesn't. In most cases it means engaging in enjoyable activity. To enjoy what you are doing is to be thoroughly absorbed in it. This is what Aristotle has in mind when he says that pleasure is not a "perceptible process" but "unimpeded activity." To be absorbed in an activity is to engage in it for its own sake, to regard it as a source of interest and value. If I enjoy restoring antiques, this means that I find the activity full of interest and worth engaging in irrespective of what other benefits, such as money, it may bring. But this is to say that the activity itself has value, independently of the pleasure it gives. Rather, it gives pleasure precisely *because* it has value. Aristotle elsewhere says the same thing about victory. To be victorious, and to be honoured for it, gives pleasure because these are themselves good things. Their goodness does not arise from the fact that they give pleasure.

This understanding of pleasure casts a rather different light on hedonism. If we take hedonism to be the instruction to seek pleasure and enjoyment, we can see that this is not the simple injunction we might have supposed. Any such advice should really be expressed in the plural: 'Seek *pleasures*'. But this leaves us with the question 'Which ones?' Aristotle, like Mill, will say 'Good ones', but unlike Mill he sees that the mark of their goodness must arise from something other than their being pleasures. At the most general level, Aristotle would say, the hedonists are right to want a pleasant life, and the most pleasant life is a happy one. The value of such a life is twofold—pleasure and happiness. But the pleasure arises from the happiness. So, if we want to know what a good life is, that is, the sort of life we ought to take pleasure in, we need to know more about happiness than pleasure.

'EUDAIMONISM' OR THE PURSUIT OF HAPPINESS

At the end of an earlier section we saw that hedonism can easily be made to generate unpalatable consequences, but that this is not enough to show it to be false. What we have now seen is that hedonism does indeed present us with a false ideal of the good life, since either it bids us aim at something very limited and not especially desirable—either a life of low-level physical gratification commended by the Cyrenaics or the refined but not very exciting pleasures of the Epicureans—or else at something unattainable—pleasure in the abstract.

These defects emerge from Aristotle's analysis, but it would be quite wrong to think that Aristotle rejected hedonism outright. On the contrary, Aristotle agreed with the hedonists in thinking pleasure highly desirable. Their mistake lay in a confusion about just what sort of thing pleasure is. They thought of it as an experience of a special kind produced by some activities, whereas it is really enjoyment of an activity itself. In the light of this erroneous conception, they further thought that the pleasure produced explains the value of the activity, just as the pain caused by some activities explains their disvalue. On Aristotle's account, the truth is quite the reverse. Things are not valuable because they give pleasure, but rather they give pleasure because and insofar as we value them. When it comes to the good life, then, the focus of our attention should not be 'hedos', pleasure or enjoyment, but what is likely to make life most pleasurable, namely 'eudaimonia', a Greek word normally translated 'happiness.'

Eudaimonia, though usually rendered 'happiness', is in some ways better translated 'well-being', for it carries with it the idea not so much of passive contentment, but active flourishing. The happy man, on Aristotle's picture, is not the man who is merely quite content with his lot, whatever it happens to be, but the man who excels at all those activities and aptitudes which are characteristic of human beings—someone with healthy appetites, an educated mind, skill in the conduct of personal and public relationships, and a wide range of friends and admirers. It is this concept of happiness that we must now explore.

MAN AS A FUNCTIONING ANIMAL

For Aristotle, man is simply one type of animal. This is indeed true, however liable we are to forget it. Given this fact, we might expect to learn something about ourselves by considering our place in the natural world. We can do this by seeing that the question 'What is a good life?' can be asked for a wide range of living things. Consider, for instance, the humble case of a potted plant. We know that there are conditions under which plants flourish and others under which they wither and die—too much or too little moisture, too much or too little light, too warm or too cold. Furthermore, just what these conditions are differ according to the type of plant—conditions that suit a cactus will not suit a tropical orchid. From this, it follows that we can say that there are good and bad living conditions for plants.

In a similar way, animals sicken and die under different conditions—a horse cannot live on meat, a lion cannot live on oats, a fish cannot live on land, a bird cannot survive under the water. But the good life for an animal is not just a matter of survival. A plant or an animal might survive, but in a weak, sickly, or malformed condition. We must speak of flourishing as well as survival if we are to distinguish what it is for a plant or animal to live well. And the conditions under which a plant or an animal flourishes we can call, along with Aristotle, the 'good' for that thing. A regime in which a lion, for instance, has the right amounts of the right sort of food, exercise, and company, will produce a lion that is both physically in excellent shape, and whose behaviour is just what is natural to lions. Conversely, as we know from the treatment of animals in zoos and circuses, if a lion is caged, isolated from other lions, and fed without having to hunt, its physique will deteriorate and its behaviour become neurotic.

In just the same fashion, Aristotle thought that we could discover the good for man. That is to say, it is possible to delineate the activities in which human beings can flourish, i.e., be best in the things that it is natural for human beings to do and be, and the conditions that make this possible. In this way, Aristotle arrives at a view of the good life importantly different from that of his predecessors. Whereas the hedonists and Plato looked for the one thing that was good above all else and good in itself (though, of course, each came up with a very different answer and further differed about how 'the good' was related to 'the good life'), Aristotle's view carries the implication that there is no one good, that what is and what is not good must always be relativized to some creature or other. What is good for a horse is not what is good for a lion, and so on indefinitely, including what is good for a human being. The good, then, is not some abstract object or property that, as it were, radiates its goodness independently of human beings and other creatures. Rather, it is a mode of existence determined by the natures of different creatures. At the same time, to make good *relative* in this way is not to make it *subjective* in the manner of Callicles, Thrasymachus, and so on, because whether something is or is not good for a horse, or a lion, or a sycamore tree is a matter of ascertainable *fact*. We cannot *decide* that oats are good for a lion, because lions either do or do not flourish on a diet of oats.

THE GOOD FOR HUMAN BEINGS

What then *is* the good life for a human being? In the *Nicomachean Ethics*, it is said to be "activity of the soul in accordance with virtue", a pious sounding expression scarcely illuminating as it stands. Its meaning, however, is actually not so hard to discern. Despite the initial impression, this phrase may make on modern minds, Aristotle's conception of the good life for a human being has in fact almost nothing to do with religion or morality as we normally understand them. 'The soul' as the term is used here is really the mind or rational faculty which human beings possess, and 'in accordance with virtue' means 'in the best possible way'. Consequently, Aristotle's conception of the good life is one in which we use our minds to make and act and think in the best possible ways. This is, of course, the good life in the abstract. It needs to be given content by appeal to the actual nature of human beings.

It is important to stress here that Aristotle's appeal to the activities of the mind does not imply that intellectual endeavour or academic inquiry makes up the good life. Rather, it is intelligence in the full range of human activities that makes for a good life, intelligence of the sort that potters, politicians, and parents may employ in their respective tasks and occupations, no less than scientists and philosophers. Indeed, Aristotle puts *phronesis*, or practical wisdom, rather than intellectual brilliance at the heart of a good life, because even the highest forms of intellectual inquiry need to be guided by good sense if they are to be pursued fruitfully and well.

The picture of the ideal human life that emerges from Aristotle's conception of the good is a moderate rather than an heroic one. It must strike us as sound and sensible rather than inspiring. Aristotle thinks that those who can be shown to lead good lives are middle-aged, educated, financially well established, socially respected. Neither slaves nor the poor or ignorant or stupid could lead good lives, for to be any of these things is to be stunted as a human being, much in the way that a tree may be stunted or an animal deformed. Moreover, those who single-mindedly pursue some one goal or strive to excel in just one thing—sport, music, or politics, say—to the detriment of prosperity, friends, family, social standing, or a rounded education, also lead impoverished lives.

One implication of Aristotelianism—that the lives of the poor and slaves are not good and that the good life is the preserve of the reasonably rich and talented and powerful— sometimes has an offensive ring to modern ears. This is because in the contemporary world the expression 'the good life' has a moral connotation (to be discussed in a later chapter) which it did not have for Aristotle. His conception implies only what most people would agree upon, that it is better to be free than to be someone else's slave, better to live in reasonable prosperity than in poverty, better to be talented (or at least accomplished) in some things than in nothing. These judgements, for Aristotle, are not fundamental moral or evaluative opinions with which others may or may not agree. Nor are they the expression of subjective preferences such as form the basis of egoism, or even natural preferences of the kind to which the hedonists appealed. Rather, they are statements of *fact*. This raises our next question, 'On what are these "facts" based?'

ETHICS AND ETHOLOGY

Aristotle, in common with most Greeks, thought that everything has a *telos* or end at which it naturally aims, and that, depending upon the mode of existence of the thing in question, this end will be reached more or less badly. Thus 'oak tree' is the end or *telos* of every acorn, and, given the right conditions, an acorn will develop into a tree of a certain shape, size, colour, and so on. Given abnormal conditions, it will deviate from this end—be stunted or deformed in some way. All this follows from the biological nature of the acorn, something about which we think we now know a lot more than Aristotle did. But though we are here concerned with the biology of the acorn and its cultivation, to speak in this way is already to refer to 'right conditions' and employ evaluative terms like 'stunted' and 'deformed'. And this gives us a clue to answering the question. Facts about right and wrong, good and bad, on Aristotle's account, are derived from facts about the biology of things. Thus, our knowledge of good is a function of our biological knowledge.

Aristotle was truly an intellectual giant and his own biological knowledge was highly advanced for his time. He thought that each species, including man, has a distinctive, and discoverable function, i.e., a *telos* peculiar to that species, and from that *telos* we can derive the good for that thing. Under the inspiration of this conception, Aristotle himself produced work that made him both the founding father of biology and the major influence upon its development for centuries to come. But more recent biology, especially since Darwin, has made such advances that, however great in its own day, Aristotelian biology has now been completely superseded. Does this mean that the ethical and evaluative implications of Aristotelianism are outmoded also?

For a good many years, it was thought so. This is because modern biology no longer believes in the existence of species that have been distinct from the beginning of creation but rather in the evolutionary emergence of species over time. Furthermore, biologists no longer see any sense in studying the physiological character of plants and animals in terms of overall function. In modern biology, we can describe the function of some part of the anatomy—the function of the heart in the anatomy of a lion, for instance—but we cannot sensibly talk about the function of the lion as a whole. The heart serves an end in the body of the lion, but the lion does not serve any end. Even if we are able to detect characteristic patterns of behaviour in lions, modern biology holds that the explanation of these will be found not in some *telos* towards which all lions naturally strive but in some genetic structure with which they begin. Thus, modern biology, rather than pointing us towards the study of individual species with a view to discovering their distinctive function, points us to the study of microbiological structure which the members of many different species share.

It seems, then, that modern biology is not the sort of study that could allow us to derive facts about right and wrong, good and bad, in the way that Aristotelian biology could. And yet Aristotelianism has undergone something of a revival in recent years. This is because alongside biology there has grown up a study much closer to Aristotle's and which may allow us to speak in some of the ways that he did. This is the study of ethology. The very name 'ethology' indicates the connexions of this relatively new science with the concerns of the ancient Greeks, because it is derived via Latin from Greek words meaning the study and depiction of character. In its modern sense, ethology can be described as the study of animal behaviour in a natural environment. Among its most famous exponents is Konrad Lorenz, who made a celebrated study of wolves.

If we set ourselves to study not the physiology but the behaviour of animals in their natural environment, we come to see, ethologists tell us, that there are conditions under which animals cannot thrive and in which their natural behaviour may undergo destructive and self-destructive alteration. For instance, the male of one species of fish possesses a sting which it uses to protect the egg-carrying female from predators. But if we remove a male and female to the safety, but confinement, of a small tank in which there are no predators, the male will eventually turn its sting upon the female herself. This behaviour is clearly abnormal since it works to the destruction of the fish and their progeny, and it arises from the unnatural conditions in which they have been placed. These conditions are simply not good for the fish.

Examples of this sort can be multiplied without difficulty. What they all show is that, though biology has no use for the idea of the natural function of a creature any more, the modern science of ethology still allows us to talk of normal and abnormal, right and wrong, good and bad, in just the way that Aristotelian biology did. More important, its judgements of right and wrong, etc., are based upon the scientific study of animals, not their biological structure but their behaviour patterns. This lends new substance to the idea that 'the good life' can be a matter of discoverable fact.

THE NATURAL AND THE NORMAL

Can scientific ethology be extended to human beings? Many ethologists have thought so and have made studies of human beings of a similar kind to those that have been made of animals. Desmond Morris's *The Naked Ape* is one of the most famous of these. Obviously, if the ethology of human beings *is* possible, and the parallel between modern ethology and Aristotelian biology holds, we have indeed discovered a way of answering the question, 'What is the good life for human beings?' Unfortunately, once we begin to think about the matter more carefully, a number of important difficulties emerge.

Ethology is defined as the study of the behaviour of animals in their natural environment, and this definition raises the first question, 'What is the natural environment of man?' We know that human beings live in strikingly different environments—compare the environment of the Inuit of the Arctic Circle with that of the Kalahari dwellers—and that their modes of existence can also differ enormously—compare the life of a New York stockbroker with that of an East African tribesman, for example, or the life of a Trappist monk with that of the promiscuous socialite. Which of these, if any, is the natural environment and which the natural mode of existence in which normal human behaviour is to be studied?

On this question the reactions of ethologists on the one hand and ordinary people on the other tend to diverge. Ethologists are generally persuaded that the behaviour of human beings can be studied profitably in all of these environments and life-styles, and that the result of such study is the revelation of interesting underlying patterns. By contrast, many ordinary people and popular writers have a strong inclination to contend that some of these environments and life-styles are in fact unnatural. It is commonplace to hear the 'naturalness' of the life of the North American Indian of old contrasted with the 'artificiality' of the life of the commuter in a modern city, for instance, or the nuclear family contrasted unfavourably with the more 'natural' extended family. From the point of view of the evaluative implication of ethology, both responses are interesting and need to be considered in turn.

Suppose the ethologists are right in thinking that human beings are equally well suited to a wide variety of environments and life-styles, and that in each of these we may detect the ways in which human behaviour characteristically displays itself. Since there are, notwithstanding the underlying similarities, marked differences between these styles of life however, we can still raise the question, 'Which is the best way of living? Which is the good life?' But this cannot now be answered by ethological study. Since ethology shows them to be equally good as far as the underlying nature of human beings is concerned, it can give us no reason to discriminate between one style of life and another. Of course, someone might argue that since scientific ethology gives us no reason to distinguish between the value of the life of the Trappist monk and the promiscuous socialite, there *is* no difference of any importance. Both ways of life are equally good. But this is not a very satisfactory conclusion. Faced with a choice between the two, I can still ask, 'Which way should I choose to live my life?' Until we have been shown that there is no answer to this question, ethological ethics which gives none, must be held to be deficient as a guide to the good life.

It ought to be stressed, perhaps, that ethologists themselves have not often been concerned to derive evaluative or ethical implications from their studies. These implications have been drawn more frequently by those who want to popularize ethology. But as I noted before, the popularizers and the ethologists very often part company on one important point, their willingness to declare some environments and styles of life 'unnatural'. The effect of this is that popular ethology is *not* silent on a lot of questions we may raise about the relative desirability of a given style of life—breast-feeding, whole foods, and the extended family are 'natural'; celibacy, food additives, and nuclear power are not. The difficulty is, however, that since scientific ethology is silent on most of these matters, however enthusiastic the popularizers, there does not seem any good basis for making the distinction between the natural and the unnatural in one way rather than another.

HOMOSEXUALITY: A TEST CASE

The question before us is whether we can usefully use the concepts of natural and unnatural to help us discriminate between good and bad ways of living. That something of this sort can be done is an assumption of quite a lot of everyday moral thinking. Some fifty years ago, it would have been common for people to describe homosexual relations as 'unnatural', and mean thereby to condemn them, or at least express disapproval. Nor was this a passing view of the matter. The greatest philosopher and theologian of Christianity in the Middle Ages, St Thomas Aquinas (who was much influenced by Aristotle), also brought unnaturalness as a charge against homosexuality and other practices he regarded as contrary to the natural law as ordained by God.

Here we need to look more closely at what 'natural' and 'unnatural' mean. In what sense is homosexuality unnatural? If by unnatural we mean 'not found in nature', the charge is false. Homosexuality *is* found in nature; that is why a question of its rightness or wrongness arises. On the other hand, if by 'unnatural' we mean 'abnormal', either we are doing no more than observing that homosexual inclination and behaviour is less common than heterosexual (i.e., is *statistically* abnormal). Or else in calling it abnormal we are just asserting that it is improper and are not actually giving a reason or explaining anything, since 'abnormal' here just means 'deviates from the norm'.

This last interpretation obviously makes 'unnatural' worthless as a basis upon which to criticise a way of living. But it has sometimes been argued that there is more to it than this. Homosexuality is abnormal because sexual activity has a natural function, the generation of offspring, which homosexual activity cannot serve. Homosexual sex is a perversion, on this view, because it is a turning away of the sexual act from its natural function.

Now this is certainly a more substantial account of what might be meant by 'natural' and 'unnatural' sex. But is it defensible? Clearly, one natural function of sex is the procreation of children, and equally clearly homosexual sex cannot serve this end. But we should not suppose that this is the only end that sex can usefully serve. It can also supply physical stimulus and psychological strengthening, and these may well have served the evolutionary development of humankind (and other animals). We need not be in a position to assert that this actually is the case, however. To see that this *could* be the case is enough to show that an appeal to natural functions cannot settle the argument about homosexuality.

It should be stressed that this appeal to arguments about homosexuality has not been made with the purpose of settling or even engaging in the dispute. The argument against homosexuality is important here as one example of the failure of appeals to 'natural' ways of living and behaving. It cannot supply us with uncontentious grounds for declaring a mode of human existence good or bad. There are many other good examples of how appeals to what is 'natural' always fail in one of the ways outlined once we begin to think about what 'natural' means. A 'natural' diet, for instance, cannot be shown to enjoy any special relationship to our biological nature or our environment. When people speak of a 'natural' diet, they often have it in mind to condemn what are called 'junk' foods. Now there may be many reasons for recommending foods high in fibre and low in fat, but that these are 'natural' cannot be one of them. First, many people 'naturally', i.e., left to their own devices, unthinkingly choose junk food. Second, it is not universally true that such diets lead to death or ill health, and, conversely, 'healthy' eaters can die young. Third, and most important, the relationship between those who choose a 'healthy' diet and the food they eat cannot be construed along the same lines as the relationship between a tiger and the animals it hunts, still less that between a plant and the nutrients it extracts from the earth and the atmosphere. There is a crucial difference. Human beings can and do take thought about what they should eat and drink. They are not driven by natural instinct alone, nor, in adult life, does it drive them very much. So, while a cow will simply turn away from meat, we can *decide* whether or not to eat it. In deciding we can certainly take into account the fact that this food serves some useful biological function, but we can take other factors into account, too, such as its *taste*. All human beings do this in fact. It is fashionable to suppose that less industrialized societies have more 'natural', additive-free, diets. In fact, poor peasants in the remotest parts of India and China add a wide variety of spices to their food. This serves many purposes, no doubt, but one of them is the enhancement of taste, an enhancement which their children have to overcome their 'natural' reactions to learn to like.

The philosophical point of this example is this. We take to some foods more easily than others. Some of these foods serve certain biological ends. Both facts are important in considering what to eat, and there may be some reason to call a diet that gives them pride of place 'natural'. However, these are not the only facets of food that we can reasonably consider in constructing our diet. Nor are we obliged by nature or by anything else to lend them an importance above all others. We can deliberate about the merits of 'natural' foods. This point can be generalized. There may be patterns of behaviour and ways of life that we have *some* reason to call natural (heterosexual activity *could* be one, though as my argument implied, I don't think it *is* one). But from this fact, if and when it is one, nothing automatically follows about the good life. We can ask ourselves critically how much weight we are to give to it.

IS THE 'GOOD FOR MAN' GOOD?

In these last examples, 'natural' has been taken to mean in part things that we unthinkingly incline towards. The possibility of raising critical questions about what comes naturally, in this sense, is in fact a very important one. So far we have been concerned to wonder whether the Aristotelian philosophy of *eudaimonism*, supplemented by popularized ethology, can provide us with an adequate conception of the good life. We have found it to be wanting in something like the way that egoism was wanting. Despite its recourse to scientifically established fact, it cannot actually give us grounds for deciding between the wide range of life-styles that we may find ourselves presented with. This is because it cannot single out just one form of life as 'naturally' good for human beings, and even if it could, this would only be one consideration amongst others. But now we have been brought to a more profound criticism. Perhaps the way of life to which we take naturally is something whose attractions we have reason to resist. Perhaps, some of the things that are good for human beings are not in fact good, viewed from a wider perspective.

For example, it may well be natural for human beings to hunt, and natural for them to take a real pleasure in the suffering and destruction of other animals. There is enough support for cruel sports in almost all times and cultures to suggest that the appetite for them, if not universal, is certainly widespread. Moreover, it is not difficult to imagine a story that explains how blood lust of this sort has evolutionary advantages and hence is part of our evolved nature. But it is just as easy to see that from the point of view of the other animals involved, or from the detached point of view that concerns itself with pain and suffering wherever these are to be found, this impulse in human beings, however natural or good for *them*, is not to be applauded or encouraged.

Similarly, I do not find it hard to imagine that ethology might show racism or xenophobia to be deeply entrenched in the unself-conscious behaviour of human beings (there seems plenty of evidence for it). Nor do I think, if such were found to be the case, that we would for long lack a plausible explanation of its place in our evolutionary development. But in such an event we would not necessarily have found reason to commend this natural human impulse, or to cease to strive against its manifestation.

In short, even if, after the fashion of Aristotle and with the assistance of ethology, we could outline with reasonable certainty and clarity a manner of life which we had reason to call the 'good for human beings', we would be left with the question whether we ought to live this way. Is the 'good for man' *good?* To put the issue like this is to separate two questions that have so far been run together, namely, 'What is a good life?' and 'What is good?' But the two questions are connected. One answer to the first is that the good life consists in realizing the good. This is our next topic.

NATURAL GOOD AND FREEDOM

At first it may sound implausible to think that what is natural to human beings—the conditions under which they thrive and the activities they unreflectively delight in—might nonetheless be an unworthy way for them to live. In fact, it is an idea with which we are quite familiar. The Christian doctrine of original sin, for instance, holds that our basic inclination is to evil. For the moment, however, we should notice another objection. Human nature and the natural are *given*. That is to say, our nature and what is natural to us is something we discover, with the help of ethology or some other science. It is a matter of fact, and from the point of view of Aristotle and many of the ancient Greeks this is one of the things that makes it a fitting basis for a conception of the good life.

But from another point of view, the one we will consider next, this is just what makes human nature and the natural an unsuitable basis for human action. This is because to appeal to facts about our nature and try to make them unalterable determinants of the way we live is to disguise from ourselves a fundamental feature of the human condition, namely its radical freedom. Faced with an account of the 'natural' way of life we are still free to choose it or reject it.

To see the full force of this point consider the position of zookeepers responsible for the health and welfare of the animals in their charge. We can well imagine that they would find ethological studies of great value, since those studies could be expected to tell them the sorts of conditions under which their animals would flourish. They might even tell them (as in the case of polar bears) that some animals simply cannot flourish in the conditions zoos can provide. In the light of this knowledge, the zookeepers will lay down a pattern of life for the different animals, which the animals will unreflectively follow (or be made to follow) and which, if the ethologists have got it right, will be good for them. The animals themselves, however, are not involved in either the discovery or the implementation of the regimen that is good for them. Nor could they be.

It should be obvious that ethology could not stand in the same relation to the life of human beings. The very simple reason is that, were such a way of life to be laid down for us, we would still have to decide whether or not to follow it. Either that, or some political 'zookeepers', who thought that their knowledge of human nature and the natural was superior, and for that reason authoritative, would deny us the freedom to choose. More importantly still, if we ourselves were to suppose that what is natural for us is authoritative, we would be denying our own freedom to choose.

One way of making this point is is to say that we would

be making our essence determine our existence, whereas existence comes before essence. This rather aphoristic remark needs a lot explanation. Briefly, it means that, as centres of consciousness, human beings first and foremost exist. What their nature or essence is is a secondary matter. Much more needs to be said, but putting the matter in this way shows how the discussion of Aristotle and ethology eventually leads us on to discussing the next philosophy of value—existentialism.

SUGGESTED FURTHER READING

Original Sources
Virtually none of the writings of Aristippus or Epicurus survives. Our knowledge of what they thought is largely derived from
Diogenes Laertius, *The Lives of the Philosophers*
Further fragments relating to Epicurus are to be found in
A A Long and D Sedley, *The Hellenistic Philosophers*, Vol. 1
John Stuart Mill, *Utilitarianism*, chap. 2
Aristotle, *Nicomachean Ethics*, esp. book 7, chaps. 11–14

Commentaries
Richard Taylor, *Good and Evil*, chaps. 6–7
J O Urmson, *Aristotle's Ethics*

Contemporary Discussion
Alasdair MacIntyre, 'Pleasure as a reason for action', *The Monist* 1965
Mary Midgley, *Beast and Man*
Konrad Lorenz, *On Aggression*

EXISTENTIALISM: GOOD FAITH AND RADICAL FREEDOM

THE ARGUMENT SO FAR

We have been asking the question 'What sort of life is best for human beings?' We began with the rather mundane answer that the best life is one of riches and fame. But we saw that this answer confuses intrinsic values—things valuable in themselves—with merely instrumental values— things valuable only as a means to things of intrinsic value. What we need is an answer that will point us to intrinsic values, and this requirement is what led us to egoism, the doctrine that the good life consists in getting what you want, whatever that might be. This was the central topic of the first chapter, but detailed analysis showed egoism to be inadequate because it either rests upon a falsehood about the sorts of motives human beings have, or it recommends a policy of following desires without telling us which out of all the desires we can have we ought to follow. If, in order to answer this objection, egoism is amended to a version that recommends the pursuit of those desires which are in my own interests, this still leave us asking just which desires *are* in my own interests.

It is at this point that hedonism may be appealed to as a supplement to egoism: follow those desires that give you plea- sure. This was the topic of Chapter Two and once again we discovered problems and difficulties. There just does not seem any reason to give a specially important place in our lives to pleasure straightforwardly construed. Indeed, there appear to be a great many aspects of a human life other than the pleasure it contains that can contribute substantially to its value.

Just what are these other aspects and how might we hope to knit them into a coherent whole? This is the question Aristotle expressly addresses and he tries to answer it by giving an account of what is distinctively human, and thus what sort of life suits human beings best. The arguments considered in the second part of Chapter Two, however, showed that the attempt to give content to the idea of the good life by appealing to human nature is not successful, chiefly for two reasons. First, even with the help of modern ethology, it is impossible to specify the natural good for human beings in sufficient detail to enable us to adjudicate between competing styles of life, even those of a radically different sort. Second, even if ethological investigation were to improve to the point where we could adequately describe the good for human beings, there is no reason to think that the attributes, attitudes, and activities that might thereby be shown to contribute to the flourishing of the human species would be good in a wider sense. The conditions under which human beings do best as a species of animal might be (and probably are) conditions under which a wide range of other creatures, both plant and animal, might be put at risk. They may also be conditions in which individuals, especially the weak, handicapped, or infirm would suffer considerably. What comes naturally to human beings and what leads to the vigorous flowering of the species has its dark side (as the Christian doctrine of original sin holds). In the absence of further argument, we have no reason to regard this dark side as an aspect of life which it would be good to promote.

KIERKEGAARD AND THE
ORIGINS OF EXISTENTIALISM

But there is another basis on which appeals to human nature as a guide to life and action may be criticized. This is their *essential* inadequacy. Some philosophers have held that no theory of human nature can ever supply an answer to the question 'How should I live?' because, presented with any such theory I still have to decide whether to accept it as a guide to life. In other words, no objectively grounded answer to practical questions of value can have the authority to command or compel my assent.

This observation is in fact the ground upon which an alternative conception of the best human life—existentialism— is founded. To speak in this way, however, may be to give the misleading impression that existentialism is a single philosophical conception. There are many existentialist writers not all of whom are philosophers, and many of whom differ radically in the views they hold. What holds them together is not uniformity of opinion so much as a common ancestry. Modern day existentialists are all concerned with problems that first seized the attention of thinkers and writers in the nineteenth century, and though different thinkers arrive at different conclusions, to a large extent they employ a common vocabulary. Even so, it is difficult to generalize about existentialist writers. In the space of a short chapter, the best we can do is consider existentialism as it is elaborated by one or two of its best-known exponents.

The writer whose themes have been acknowledged by existentialist writers as formative was an obscure nineteenth-century Dane, Søren Kierkegaard. Kierkegaard was a very curious man as well as a prolific writer, but his fame is chiefly as a religious thinker rather than as a theologian in the normal sense. By upbringing and persuasion, he was a Protestant Christian, and for a time aspired to be a country parson. Nonetheless, he reacted sharply to many of the features of the Danish Lutheran church of his day. This reaction was volubly expressed in a large number of writings. However, he was also reacting to the philosophy dominant in Northern Europe in the early and middle nineteenth century, namely, the philosophy of one of Berlin's most famous professors, G W F Hegel.

Kierkegaard's objections to established Lutheranism and to Hegelian philosophy were at bottom the same. To his mind, both, in different ways, tried to make the demands of Christianity reasonable. In the case of the church, the Gospel was presented, not as a radical challenge to the customary intellectual and social order of the world, but as the sort of thing that reasonable and respectable men and women would naturally agree to. He instances the biblical story of Abraham and Isaac. In that story, Abraham, under the belief that God requires it of him, is represented as willing to take an innocent child, his own son, and murder him, though in the end the boy lives. Kierkegaard was stuck by the fact that church people could listen to this story with attention and respect, whereas, if one of their neighbours actually acted in the way that Abraham did, they would be scandalized. Similarly, in the mouths of Protestant pastors all trace of the mystery of the Trinity or the absurdity of the Incarnation was smothered by sheer respectability, till both doctrines lost anything that could be called challenging. On Kierkegaard's view,

it behooves us to get rid of introductory guarantees of security, proofs from consequences, and the whole mob of public parsons and guarantors, so as to permit the absurd to stand out in all its clarity—in order that the individual may believe if he wills it . . . [because Christianity] has proclaimed itself as the Paradox, and it has required of the individual the inwardness of faith in relation to that which stamps itself as an offence to the Jews and folly to the Greeks—and an absurdity to the understanding. (*Concluding Unscientific Postscript*, pp. 190–91).

In the case of Hegel, the transformation of the Christian Gospel was more self-conscious. Hegel claimed that his philosophical system, with which he aimed to encompass and explain all aspects of human knowledge and experience, was nothing less than an encyclopaedic rationalization of the Christian religion. It was the truth of Christianity converted into a form to which all rational minds could assent. To Hegel, to accomplish such a transformation was to do Christianity a great service, to put it beyond the vagaries of 'faith' or mere subjective opinion. But to Kierkegaard it was nothing short of its destruction. To make Christianity 'rational' was to turn it into a mere theory which might elicit our intellectual assent but which did not demand and could not sustain what Kierkegaard called the 'inwardness' which real religious faith requires.

Moreover, on Kierkegaard's view, the Hegelian 'System' (which he mocks by spelling with a capital S) is worthless as a guide to life. To try to respond to the question 'How shall I live?' by following a philosophical system is "like travelling in Denmark with the help of a small map of Europe, on which Denmark shows no larger than a steel pinpoint" (*Concluding Unscientific Postscript*, p. 275). Philosophical systems are too lofty, too far removed from practical living, to be of any use. The trouble with speculative metaphysicians like Hegel, he tells us in another place, is that they must turn aside from their contemplation of space and time in order to blow their nose!

Kierkegaard's writings are full of this sort of remark, and they abound in paradox. Much of what he writes is suggestive, but it is difficult to reconstruct Kierkegaard's polemic into a consistent and sustained intellectual critique of academic philosophy. Partly this is because he wanted to avoid all systematic philosophizing. Many of his books he wrote under a variety of pseudonyms, intending them to be the presentation of differing, sometimes conflicting, points of view. At the same time, there are elements that are puzzlingly inconsistent. For instance, his analogy of the map suggests that philosophical systems are the right *sort* of thing (a guide) but on the wrong scale. In countless other places, what Kierkegaard writes implies that philosophy, or any form of thought which aims to arrive at demonstrable conclusions, is the wrong kind of thinking by which try to address the fundamental questions of human existence.

Understanding Kierkegaard is further complicated by his insistence that we cannot grasp thought in independence of the person whose thought it is. There is a unity of living and thinking which must be appreciated if we are to understand an author. In Kierkegaard's case, this introduces another element of paradox. His writings are of a highly individualistic, anti-conventional character. Yet to outward appearances his life was no more remarkable than most of his middle-class Danish contemporaries. He lived quietly on a private income inherited from his father, and, apart from a broken engagement and an unpleasant brush with the press later in life, there is nothing about his life that could be called historic or dramatic.

Still, for all this confusing abundance, Kierkegaard's writings contain certain abiding themes. In his earlier writings, he describes three different ways of life—the aesthetic, the ethical, and the religious. These are represented as mutually exclusive, and requiring the individual to make a radical choice between them. It is in the later writings, notably *Concluding Unscientific Postscript*, that the philosophical underpinnings of this requirement are set out. Three of these form the basis of the existentialist point of view. First, the most fundamental questions facing a human being are essentially practical because the question 'How shall I spend my life?' is inescapable. Whatever interest there may be in purely intellectual questions, they can never take priority over practical questions of living. This is something it is especially important to grasp in the context of religion. Christianity (or any other religion) is a way of living, not a theoretical explanation of the world or of human experience. It follows from this that it is a deep mistake to try to substitute a theological doctrine or a philosophical system for a religious faith.

Speculative philosophy is objective, and objectively there is no truth for existing individuals, but only approximations; for the existing individual is precluded from becoming altogether objective by the fact that he exists. (*Concluding Unscientific Postscript*, p. 201)

It is perfectly true, as philosophers say [for instance, Hegel in *The Philosophy of Right*], that life must be understood backwards. But they forget the other proposition, that it must be lived forwards. (*Journals*, sect. 127)

Second, it is not only fruitless but misleading to try to demonstrate or prove the objective truth of the beliefs by which men and women are expected to live. This is because in matters of living, as opposed to questions of pure intellect (natural science for instance), 'truth is subjectivity'. What Kierkegaard means by this is that any religion or philosophy which we are meant to live by has actually *to be lived by*. This means that whatever the objective truth of the matter, those who live by it have to accept its truth subjectively, that is, as true for them. Between the presentation of a doctrine and its acceptance by those to whom it is presented, there is an essential and inescapable gap, which cannot be closed by still further intellectual investigation, evidence, or proof, but only by a subjective 'leap of faith'. (It is from Kierkegaard that this familiar expression comes.)

But, thirdly, though from the point of view of critical objectivity the 'truth which edifies' will always appear 'absurd', this does not imply that we are free to live by any old doctrine that takes our fancy. The attainment of practical, subjective truth is as at least as difficult as the intellectual effort involved in speculative theory.

The realm of faith is not a class for numskulls in the sphere of the intellectual, or an asylum for the feeble-minded. Faith constitutes a sphere all by itself. (*Concluding Unscientific Postscript*, p. 291)

The effort involved in the attainment of faith, however, is emotional rather than intellectual. Kierkegaard wrote several books with titles like *Fear and Trembling, The Concept of Dread*, and *Purity of Heart*, and he had a great deal to say in general about the emotional conditions under which a real living faith emerges. On his view,

there is only one proof of the truth of Christianity and that, quite rightly, is from the emotions, when the dread of sin and a heavy conscience torture a man into crossing the narrow line between despair bordering upon madness—and Christendom. (*Journals*, sect. 926)

Kierkegaard's overriding concern was with religious faith and with the demands of Christianity in particular. This emphasis upon Christianity continues to make him of interest as a religious writer. But many of the central elements in his thought can in fact be given a wholly secular treatment. Though some later existentialists have also been Christians, the most famous existentialist of all, the French philosopher Jean Paul Sartre, was avowedly atheist. As we shall see, however, despite this important difference the fundamentals of his thought are strikingly similar to Kierkegaard's.

SARTRE AND RADICAL FREEDOM

It is Sartre who uses the expression "existence comes before essence." This is a summation of what it is that all existentialists, Christian and non-Christian, have in common. What it means is that in answering the basic question of existence, 'How should I live?' we must reject any appeal to the idea of human nature, that is to say, any appeal to a conception of 'human being' that will be found in every individual and of which each individual is an example. Part of the reason for rejecting this conception is the belief that human beings have no pre-ordained, essential character. "Man is nothing else but what he makes of himself" (*Existentialism and Humanism*, p. 28).

There is no such thing as human nature on Sartre's view,

because there is no God who created it. The only coherent way in which we can speak of a distinctive human nature is as a preconceived creative plan for human beings, similar to the plan an engineer may form for a particular design of engine. Such a design—the essential character of the engine—precedes the existence of any actual engine, and each engine is a realization of that design. If there were a God, and he had conceived of human beings and then created them, we could speak of human nature, and could even say that human essence comes before existence. But there is no God and hence no preordained human nature.

Of course, if this were all there were to Sartre's argument, he could hardly claim that existentialists, both religious and nonreligious, share the common ground he claims. For it would amount to no more than an assertion of the truth of atheism, an assertion Christians and others would equally deny. But Sartre also argues that, even if there were a creative God with a preformed plan for human beings, there would still be an unmistakable sense in which existence must come before essence. This is because, like Kierkegaard, Sartre thinks that the question of existence is more a practical than a metaphysical matter.

In the lecture *Existentialism and Humanism*, Sartre, too, uses the biblical example of Abraham and Isaac to bring this out. In that story, an angel commands Abraham to sacrifice his son Isaac on an altar. Were we to treat the story in a purely objective mood as a piece of history, we would ask whether Abraham really was addressed by a supernatural voice, and no doubt many people today reject stories like this because they no longer believe in the reality of angelic voices. But Sartre sees that, even if there were no doubt about the reality of the supernatural voice, Abraham would have to decide whether or not it was the voice of an angel, a real messenger from God, or only an imposter albeit a supernatural one. And this is a question that only he can decide.

In a similar way, each one of us is addressed personally by the claims of God, or an ethical demand.

If a voice speaks to me, it is still I myself who must decide whether the voice is or is not that of an angel. If I regard a certain course of action as good, it is only I who choose to say that it is good and not bad." (*Existentialism and Humanism*, p. 33)

Thus, any answer to the question 'How shall I live?' is inescapably existential. However authoritative, however objectively 'provable' or 'unprovable', it requires the one whose existence it addresses to give it assent. Without this, Sartre thinks, any such answer is effectively silent, and thus is no answer at all.

It is in this sense that human beings are radically free. Nothing we can imagine, no God, no human nature, and no science or philosophy, can decide for us the fundamental question of existence. Moreover, there is another side to this freedom. Because nothing determines the answer except ourselves, we alone are responsible for the decisions we make. Freedom liberates our will from the determination of any other agency, but it also leaves us solely responsible. This is why Sartre says

man is condemned to be free. Condemned, because he did not create himself, yet is nevertheless at liberty, and from the moment he is thrown into this world he is responsible for everything he does. (*Existentialism and Humanism*, p. 34)

The argument so far might be taken to imply that man's inescapable freedom is a logical truth, something we come to understand through philosophical analysis. At one level, this is true. Sartre thinks that radical freedom arises out of the nature of the human condition. "There is no difference," he says, "between the being of man and his being free" (*Being and Nothingness*, p. 25). This remark comes from his largest philosophical work, *Being and Nothingness*, in which he offers a full-scale metaphysical analysis of what it is for something to exist. There are, according to Sartre, two modes of existing, Being-in-itself and Being-for-itself. What this rather obscure terminology is meant to capture is the contrast between things, like stones and trees, that are just *there* and have no awareness of or value for themselves (Being-in-itself) and things, notably human beings, that are aware of themselves and whose consciousness of their own existence is central (Being-for-itself). The contrast also has to do with the point about past and future which Kierkegaard makes. Action, and thought about it, has to do with the future. Whereas the past is made and unalterable, the distinguishing feature of the future is that it is yet *to be* made. At present it is nothing, to be fashioned as we will.

It is the peculiarity of human beings that they are *both* physical objects (and thus Being-in-itself), *and* consciousnesses (and hence Being-for-itself). But the distinctive feature of Being-for-itself, or consciousness, is that it is a sort of nothingness, just in the sense that it can never be or become simply another object in the world. No matter how hard we try to think of ourselves as merely physical objects existing alongside all the other objects of the world, our consciousness always floats free, so to speak. It is always a *subject*, never an *object*. The point may be illuminated by this parallel. In order to have visual experience of anything, we need literally to occupy some point of view. But the point of view we occupy, though essential to sight, cannot itself figure as an object within the visual field. If I stand on a hillside, my position determines my field of vision. It is not within that field. If we are to see things at all, occupying some point of view is crucial. But the point of view is not itself something seen, and could not be. So, too, with the subject of consciousness. Subjective consciousness is an ineliminable precondition for the perception and understanding of objects, but never itself an object. It is not a *thing* at all.

Many people find this sort of philosophical analysis hard to understand and appreciate. Sartre himself did not suppose that his analysis would by itself be illuminating because he regarded the inescapability of freedom not merely as a conclusion from metaphysical analysis but as an actual feature of lived human experience. For this reason, much of his thinking about freedom is to be found in novels rather than in formal philosophical works. In these novels, different characters come to a deepening realization of just what a gulf there is between the way in which ordinary objects exist and the way in which human beings exist. As a result of this sort of reflection, they come to appreciate what it means to be free.

The experience is not a pleasant one but one of anguish, since radical freedom is a difficult and painful condition to accept. This idea of an anguish which results from a true perception of the human condition is not dissimilar to Kierkegaard's Dread, and it has an important part to play in Sartre's philosophy of value. But in order to see this we have to go back a little.

ANGUISH AND BAD FAITH

Sartre's remark that it is I who must choose to say whether a given course of action or way of life is good or bad for me might lead us to think that each individual may do as he or she pleases. But this is not so, at least, if 'do as one pleases' means take whatever course of action is most agreeable. What is true is that a good human life is distinguished not by what is chosen, but by the manner in which it is chosen. A wholly authentic or truly human life is possible only for those who recognize the inescapability of freedom and its responsibility. (The terms 'authentic' and 'inauthentic' come from another existentialist, the German philosopher Martin Heidegger.) And this recognition can be achieved only at the cost of anguish. Consequently, a good life, the sort of life that has meaning and value, is not easy to achieve.

Anguish arises from two sources. The first is the perception that in recognizing our radical freedom as human beings we are acknowledging that we are nothing, literally *no thing*. As a result, nothing can fully determine our choice of life for us, and hence nothing can explain or justify what we are. In this rather special sense, we are absurd, and it is the absurdity of human existence that the acknowledgement of radical freedom brings with it. Sartre thinks that the existence of everything, Being-in-itself as well as Being-for-itself, is absurd. By this he means that existence is always a matter of brute, inexplicable fact. But the fact that we share our absurdity with everything else does not make us any the less absurd, or make the human condition any easier to accept. Indeed, as we shall see, Sartre spends a good deal of time exploring the ways in which human beings strive to hide from themselves their own absurdity.

The second source of anguish is this. Acknowledgement of our freedom to make choices makes us, literally, creators of the world of value, and as a consequence we bear all the responsibility which that brings with it, and this responsibility turns out to be immense.

When we say that man chooses himself, we do mean that every one of us must choose himself; but by that we also mean that in choosing for himself he chooses for all men. . . . What we choose is always the better, and nothing can be better for us unless it is better for all. If, moreover, existence precedes essence and we will to exist at the same time as we fashion our image, that image is valid for all and for the entire epoch in which we find ourselves. Our responsibility is thus much greater than we had supposed, for it concerns mankind as a whole. (*Existentialism and Humanism*, p. 29)

If Sartre is correct in this, by being radically free—that is, free not merely to respond to values but to create them—the individual, in acknowledging that freedom, takes on the responsibility of legislating for all mankind. One way of putting this would be to say that in acknowledging our radical freedom we must recognize the necessity of playing God, with the awesomeness that comes with such a thought. In fact, Sartre himself says, "To be man means to reach towards being God. Or if you prefer, man fundamentally is the desire to be God" (*Being and Nothingness*, p. 556).

A true understanding of our condition as human beings, then, involves the recognition that at bottom our existence is absurd. To say that it is absurd is to say that it is without necessity or explanation. Human existence is a matter of brute fact and it is only by adopting Godlike aspirations that we can bestow any meaning upon it. Not surprisingly, since as T S Eliot once wrote "human kind cannot bear very much reality", ordinary human beings are strongly inclined to avoid the anguish by hiding the truth from themselves. Sartre distinguishes three characteristic ways in which this is done.

The first of these strategies for avoiding anguish is the least interesting. It is the response of those who think that, faced with alternative courses of action and modes of life, they can simply fail to choose. But this is an illusion. The decision not to choose is itself a choice, and a choice for which the individual is no less responsible than any other. Indecision leads to consequences as certainly as conscious decision; inactivity is one form of activity.

The second kind of response to anguish is the way of the 'serious minded'. These are the people, often religious but not necessarily so, who assert that there *is* some objective source of value, God perhaps, or just Goodness itself, and who profess to direct their lives in accordance with this objective source of value. The hedonists and Aristotle are 'serious minded' in this sense. So are Christians, Muslims, and Jews, and any others who purport to find the source of all that is good somewhere other than in their own decisions and commitment. What such people fail to see is that the only way these objective, external values can come to guide their lives is through their own commitment to those values as values. This is the point of Kierkegaard's stress upon the necessity of subjectivity. Alternatively, such serious-minded people seek the advice of others. But even when they receive it, they have still to decide for themselves whether to accept it. And, as Sartre points out in the famous case of a young man who sought his advice during the Second World War about whether to join the Free French Army or remain at home with his mother, the choice of adviser can in itself represent a decision. Often we preselect the people whose advice we seek.

The third avenue of escape from anguish is bad faith. 'Bad faith' is perhaps modern existentialism's most famous concept, and almost as famous is the example Sartre uses to illustrate it. The idea is this: Faced with the terrifying realities of the human condition (its absurdity and responsibility), individuals may seek escape by ordering their lives according to some preordained social role. Instead of accepting their own subjectivity and freedom to choose, they may try to *objectify* themselves, adopt roles that they act out, and think of themselves as mere functionaries. Sartre's waiter is such an individual. He suppresses his personality and individuality and thinks of himself, not as the individual he is, but as *a* waiter whose every action is determined by the job. But, of course, if existential freedom is inescapable, this attempt at objectification in a social role is doomed to failure. The best the waiter can accomplish is a sort of playacting.

His movement is quick and forward, a little too precise, a little too rapid. He comes towards the patrons with a step a little too quick. He bends forward a little too eagerly; his voice, his eyes express an interest a little too solicitous for the order of the customer. Finally there he returns, trying to imitate in his walk the inflexible stiffness of some kind of automaton while carrying his tray with the recklessness of a tight-rope walker. All his behaviour seems to us a game . . . the waiter in the cafe plays with his condition in order to realize it. (*Being and Nothingness*, p. 59)

What such pretence involves is a measure of self-deception. The waiter pretends to himself that his every thought and movement is determined by what it means to be a waiter.

He applies himself to chaining his movements as if they were mechanisms, the one regulating the other; his gestures and even his voice seem to be mechanisms; he gives himself the quickness and pitiless rapidity of things. (*Being and Nothingness*, p. 59)

But in his heart of hearts he must know that the role determines his behaviour for only as long as he chooses to let it. At any moment, he can turn on his heel and leave his customers standing and their orders unfulfilled. He only pretends to himself that he cannot.

Self-pretence and self-deception are puzzling concepts. When I deceive other people I know the truth and they do not. But how then can I deceive *myself*, for this requires me both to know and not to know the truth? This is an important question, but the explanation of bad faith can make do with something less than self-deception in the fullest sense. It is enough that we can avoid reminders of the truth. The waiter knows that he could adopt a quite different attitude to those who come to his cafe, but he refuses to think about it. In a similar way, but of course with much more grievous results, some Nazi commandants assumed the role of the obedient soldier, one who simply has to accept orders, and they refused to deliberate about any alternative. To describe these cases properly, we do not need to say that those involved both knew and did not know what courses of action were open to them. We need only say that they knew but would not think about it.

Nazi commandants may or may not have acted in bad faith (there is more to be said about this shortly). Sartre's primary concern is with more mundane roles, those we adopt in an attempt to escape the anguish of radical freedom. Such attempts are futile because human freedom is inescapable. Acting in bad faith cannot accomplish what it is supposed to. Even so, it is still to be avoided since it constitutes an inauthentic way of living. This gives us a clue to the existentialist conception of the good life. It is the life lived in good faith. Though Sartre says relatively little about this ideal, we can see that it consists in the pursuit of consciously self-chosen values and purposes for which the chooser takes full responsibility. When it comes to fundamental moral and evaluative questions, Sartre states:

There are no means of judging. The content is always concrete and therefore unpredictable; it always has to be invented. The one thing that counts is to know whether the invention is made in the name of freedom. (*Existentialism and Humanism*, pp. 52–53)

EXISTENTIALISM EXAMINED

There are four principal difficulties that the existentialist philosophy of value encounters. First, we may ask whether human existence is absurd in a way that gives reason for anguish. Second, is it always, or even usually, better to act in good faith? Third, in what sense, if any, is it true that individual human beings are the creators of value? And fourth, are we really so radically free? It is best to consider each of these questions in turn.

ABSURDITY AND ANGUISH

According to Sartre and many other existentialist writers, human existence is absurd. What they mean by this is that there is no explanation of the existence of human beings in general or of any individual in particular which will show it to be necessary. All existence is a matter of brute, contingent fact. To take this view is to take sides in a long-standing philosophical dispute, one which dominated seventeenth- and eighteenth-century intellectual debate. On one side were philosophers who subscribed to what was called rationalist metaphysics, notably Descartes, Leibniz, and Spinoza. They thought that there *must* be a reason for everything's being as it is. If there were not, the world would be unintelligible, a meaningless jumble of events. This belief that everything has an explanation is often called 'the principle of sufficient reason'.

In opposition to the rationalist metaphysicians were the philosophers generally called empiricists. Among these, John Locke and David Hume are the best known. They regarded the ambition to provide a sufficient reason for everything as a profound error. The empiricists were impressed by the results of experimental science, then still in its infancy. They saw that explanations of natural facts could be obtained by experimental inquiry into empirical facts (hence the name empiricist). To explain in this way, however, was to do no more than appeal to demonstrable contingencies—how things *are*, not how they *must* be. To the empiricists, the rationalists' mistake lay in supposing that matters of scientific fact could be explained in the same way as the propositions of logic or mathematics. Logical and mathematical theories can be demonstrated by abstract reasoning to hold by necessity. Scientific theories can only be shown by experimental reasoning to hold as a matter of contingent, i.e., non-necessary fact.

When Sartre and others say that human existence is absurd, they mean to side with the empiricists and deny that it can have any rationalistic explanation. They differ from the empiricists, however, in the implications they draw from this. In seeing the absurdity of human existence as a cause of anguish, they imply that the absence of a rationalistic explanation is an unfortunate deficiency, something that we need but cannot have if we are to make sense of our lives. From an empiricist point of view, however, to think this is to share the rationalist's mistake. The mistake lies in the *aspiration* to supply a logically sufficient reason for everything. The right thing to do is abandon that aspiration. But once it has been abandoned, the fact that human existence is not the sort of thing that can be given a logically sufficient reason need not trouble us. Human existence is not a matter of logical necessity. It is a matter of contingent fact. But why should anyone want more than this?

The language of absurdity can mislead us. To conclude that human existence is absurd seems to provide some reason for despair. But if 'life is absurd' just means 'there is no logically necessary explanation of the existence of human beings', we have no reason for anguish, unless we think there should be such an explanation. According to empiricists, this is just what we ought not to think. The existentialists, it seems, have not wholly discarded the rationalism with which they find fault. This is why they are sometimes described as 'disappointed rationalists'.

If this analysis is correct, there is a serious question to be raised about the basis of existentialist philosophy, as least as it has been expounded by more recent thinkers (though some of the same points can be made about Kierkegaard). However, it would be foolish to think that these important issues could be settled with a few brief remarks. The most we can do here is raise them, and pass on to the other aspects of existentialism that ought to be examined.

IS IT BETTER TO ACT IN GOOD FAITH?

The chief implication of existentialism with respect to human conduct is this: what you choose to do, how you choose to spend your life, is not as important as the way you choose it. Whatever the choice, it is at least valuable insofar as it is made in good faith. This means it is made in full recognition of the freedom and responsibility that attach to all human choice.

The idea that value attaches to the manner and motive behind the choices we make is a very plausible one. We know, for instance, that the value of a gift can lie almost entirely in the spirit in which it is given. A gift given in bad grace may cost much more but be of far less value than a simple present more gracefully given. Similarly, an inquiry made out of nothing more than a sense of professional duty will be valued much less than the same words spoken in friendship. On a larger scale, the same thing applies. The poverty of St Francis of Assisi can be regarded as a blessing, the path to an admirable life because of the spirit in which it was accepted. But just the same degree of poverty would be a misfortune in most other lives because of the resentment and disaffection that would accompany it. What such examples show is that the motive and intention of an action and the spirit expressed in it can all be important factors in the evaluation of that action.

So much we might all agree with. But existentialists want to go further and claim, first, that the *primary* value that attaches to an action or a way of life is the mentality of those who have chosen it and, second, that, of all the possible attitudes that might be taken into consideration, it is our attitude to freedom and responsibility that matters. Often we regard upbringing, or culture, or genes, as the formative influence in determining the individual's attitudes and personality, as the things that make us who we are. To the existentialist, this is an important error. It is our own choices that determine who we are, and to pretend otherwise is bad faith. Consequently, to recognize our fundamental freedom to be self-determining is the only possible response of good faith. Such recognition is distinctively human, and for that reason good faith is the most important human achievement.

But, necessarily, to recognize our freedom to determine for ourselves what we shall be places no constraints on possible choices. This means that *any* choice might be made in good faith. To choose to be a vicious criminal could be as much an expression of good faith as choosing to devote your life to those who suffer. The question then arises as to whether the fact that a vicious life is chosen in good faith makes that life any better.

A standard example used to explore this question is that of the sincere Nazi. No doubt, many of those who served the Nazi party and Hitler's government were mere time servers, in the business solely for personal gain. Others were individuals who chose to do what they did in bad faith, disguising from themselves the truth about the regime that they were serving, or pleading the necessity of following orders. But there were undoubtedly some who were true believers, who saw in nazism a creed that they could serve, and who freely chose to endorse it. Moreover, they willingly, even gladly, accepted the responsibility for fashioning a world built upon those values, even though this implied genocide.

What are we to make of such people? This is a question that historians, novelists, and philosophers have asked repeatedly since the end of the Third Reich. The implication of existentialism seems to be that, though these people led wicked lives, the fact that they freely chose them and acknowledged their responsibility for this choice is a redeeming feature. But is it? It may be plausible to say on behalf of the sincere Nazi that at least he accepted responsibility and did not try to hide it. Is it any less plausible to think that the person who accepted his role in the Holocaust in bad faith at least had sufficiently decent feelings not positively to want to be that way?

It is difficult to know how this disagreement might be resolved. One line of thought we might adopt on behalf of the existentialist says that the life of the sincere Nazi is *objectively* bad but *subjectively* good. If this means that, though his life was bad, it embodied those things that were values for him, we can hardly deny it. He did indeed choose those values; that is what is meant by calling him sincere. But this does not advance matters. We know what he freely chose. We want to know whether the fact that he freely chose makes it better or not.

A more radical line of thought and one to which some existentialist writers have been drawn suggests that, at least in a range of cases, we cannot draw this contrast between subjective and objective value, because there only is subjective value. Kierkegaard says something like this about the decision to be a Christian.

It is subjectivity that Christianity is concerned with, and it is only in subjectivity that its truth exists, if it exists at all; objectively, Christianity has absolutely no existence. (*Concluding Unscientific Postscript*, p. 116)

In a similar vein, Sartre says:

whenever a man chooses his purpose and commitment in all clearness and in all sincerity, whatever that purpose may be it is impossible to prefer another for him. (*Existentialism and Humanism*, p. 50)

And a little later on he says:

if I have excluded God the Father, there must be somebody to invent values. (p. 54)

What this seems to imply is that, at least for a range of cases, it is wrong to think of the individual choosing between values. Rather, the act of choice itself confers value. In other words, we are ourselves creators of value. Elsewhere, it is true, Sartre says things that appear to deny this implication. It will be appropriate to consider these other remarks a little later on. For the moment we have been brought to the third critical question listed above.

ARE WE CREATORS OF VALUE?

In asking this question, we must be careful to ask who 'we' are. Once this supplementary question is raised, two importantly different positions can be distinguished. One way of interpreting the question 'Are *we* creators of value?' takes 'we' to mean a group of some sort—the particular society in which an individual lives, the general cultural milieu in which the question is raised, or even the whole human race. Taken this way, the question 'Are we creators of value?' means 'Are values pre-established for individuals by the group to which they belong, be it their race, culture, or society?' Many people, including a good many philosophers, think the answer to this question is 'yes', and the philosophy of value they thereby accept usually goes by the name of 'relativism'. This is because, understood in this way, whether something is or is not of value is a matter relative to some context. This means that questions of human value cannot be intelligibly raised in the abstract. Outside some context or other, such questions simply do not make sense. More important, since the context to which questions of value are relative is a human one, there is thus a sense in which human beings are the creators of value. It is in the context of the interests, preferences, and goals of human beings that things come to have value.

A parallel to this kind of relativism is to be found in the law. Polygamy (marriage to more than one wife) is permitted in some legal jurisdictions, notably Islamic ones, and forbidden in others, notably Christian ones. To ask in the abstract 'Is it illegal to marry two women?' is to ask a senseless question. The only answer that can be given relativizes it to a context: 'It is in England, but not in Saudi Arabia'. The question only makes sense within the context of some body of law. Within such a context, there will (usually) be a straightforward answer; outside such a context, there is no answer at all. Similarly, relativists think, all matters of value can only be discussed intelligibly within a human context, and it makes no sense to think of values as things that transcend human interests and desires.

Other philosophers (Plato, for instance) have construed matters differently and supposed that in matters of value, just as in matters of scientific fact, there is mind-independent truth waiting to be discovered. Where true value lies is a question over which the whole of mankind could be confused and mistaken. Such a position is called 'objectivism' or 'realism', because it believes in real, objective values, and not merely in that which is subjectively valuable from the point of view of mankind.

When Sartre declares that there are no independent values for the 'serious minded' to follow, and when Kierkegaard says that the truth that edifies cannot be objective, both mean to reject the Platonic or realist conception of value. This is a more radical contention than the relativism just outlined. Though there are obviously some very important differences between objectivism and relativism, it should be clear that they are equally 'objective' from the existentialist point of view. Both make matters of value true or false independent of the individual. It might be true (as relativism holds) that certain forms of sex and marriage are to be valued only because of the sorts of creatures human beings are and the kinds of social institutions that have grown up over the centuries. But, if so, this does not make these values any more a matter about which the existing individual can pick and choose than if they had been established facts before the advent of any human beings at all.

Existentialism seems to go further than this and interprets the question 'Are we creators of value?' as one referring to individuals. It means 'Is each one of us a creator of value?' Sartre likens the situation of anguished choice in which every individual is placed to that of military leaders who by ordering an attack may be sending a number of men to their death.

All leaders know that anguish. It does not prevent their acting, on the contrary it is the very condition of their action, for the action presupposes that there is a plurality of possibilities, and in choosing one of these, they realise that it has value only because it is chosen. (*Existentialism and Humanism*, p. 32)

The final part of this quotation suggests that the freedom of individuals extends beyond choosing their own values out of a preexistent set, and in some cases at least includes the freedom to *make* things valuable.

To see whether this radical version of existentialism is plausible, consider the following example. Dr Samuel Johnson the famous eighteenth-century wit and conversationalist, had some very odd physical habits.

On occasion . . . when he suddenly stopped in his tracks, he would perform with his feet and hands a series of antics so strange that a crowd would gather around him laughing or staring. As if oblivious to their presence, he would either hold out his arms with some of the fingers bent, as though he had been seized by cramp, or he would hold them high and stiff above his head, or, alternatively, close to his chest, when he would agitate them up and down in the manner of a jockey holding the reins of a horse galloping at full speed. At the same time he formed his feet into the shape of a V with either the heels together or the toes. Having twisted his limbs into the required postures, with many corrections and alterations of their relative positions, he would finally take a great leap forward and walk on with the satisfied air of a man who had performed a necessary duty and who seemed totally unconscious of having done anything odd. (Christopher Hibbert, *A Personal History of Samuel Johnson*, p. 201)

As a matter of fact, extreme mannerisms of this type are not as uncommon as we might suppose, but even so we can reasonably be puzzled by them, in Johnson or in anyone else. 'Why do this sort of thing?' we want to know.

A little girl once had the courage to ask Johnson directly and he replied gently, "From bad habit. Do you, my dear, take care to guard against bad habits" (Hibbert, p. 203). This, of course, is no real explanation at all and leaves his behaviour as mysterious as before. It is possible to imagine things that Johnson might have said that would have gone some way to explaining his behaviour. For instance, he might have replied that people's lives were dull enough and that if he could give them a little harmless amusement he was willing to spend the time and stand the cost to his reputation that this involved. No doubt we would still have questions to ask, but his story would be the start of an explanation because it would connect his behaviour with a preexistent value, namely, providing others with harmless amusement.

Suppose, however, instead of an explanation such as this, Johnson assumed the extreme existentialist point of view and said that gyrating in the manner described was something he did indeed regard as 'a necessary duty' and something to which he attached great value. Unlike the first explanation, this does not in fact make any sense of his behaviour, or give us a clue as to why he has, or we should, adopt it. Consequently, and despite his imagined assertion to the contrary, it does *not* bestow any meaning or confer value. This is because it lacks any connexion with values we can recognize.

It is of the utmost importance to stress here that *recognizing* values is not the same as *sharing* them. We may not be likely to share the desire to give harmless fun to complete strangers at our own expense, but we can recognize it as the sort of value we could have. Equally important is the observation that people can actually value things that are unintelligible or meaningless. To say that the individual cannot create values does not mean that Johnson could not really have attached importance to his little ritual. Presumably he did. What it shows is that his attachment, however deep, was not sufficient to make it valuable.

An existentialist might reply that his attachment to the ritual makes it valuable *for him*. There is reason to think Sartre would reply in this way. He expressly denies that his version of existentialism is "narrowly subjective". He wants to reject the distinction between subjective and objective and appeals instead to "inter-subjectivity", saying, "In every purpose there is universality, in this sense that every purpose is comprehensible to every man" (*Existentialism and Humanism*, p. 46). About the choice of an individual made in good faith, we can say both that it rests upon shared values and that no one but he can make it.

But to my mind this retreat from the radical position is made at the expense of clarity. There is an uninteresting sense in which only the individual can make his own choice, namely, the sense in which if anyone else made it it would not be *his*. If this is what Sartre means by its being impossible "to prefer another choice for him", we must agree. But the truth of this does not remove the possibility of saying that he ought to have chosen differently. If *this* is what Sartre means to rule out, then he has indeed embraced "narrow subjectivity".

More needs to be said, but our purpose here is not the detailed interpretation of Sartre so much as a review of general lines of thought. What we have seen is this: Faced with the phenomenon of the sincere Nazi, the existentialist must either simply assert that his good faith makes his actions better than the same action performed in bad faith would have been, an assertion many will feel inclined to deny. Or else the existentialist must argue that in some sense or other subjectivity is creative of human value. It is this claim that the example of Johnson puts to the test, and it is not easy to see how a satisfactory response to that sort of example can be devised.

The arguments we have considered both for and against the existentialist's position are thus inconclusive. For all that has been said, existentialists can continue to *assert* the individual's radical freedom from any natural or conventional values. This brings us to the fourth critical question.

ARE HUMAN BEINGS RADICALLY FREE?

The heart of existentialism is the doctrine of radical freedom. The human condition, we are told, is one of inescapable freedom (though not just this) and hence inescapable responsibility, the unceasing responsibility to choose our own values and commit ourselves to them. This idea conflicts sharply with familiar ways of speaking. We often say things like 'I cannot come because I must . . . ', and the 'cannot' and 'must' signify necessities that constrain our choices and our actions. They rule out courses of action as impossible. But if Sartre is right, such ways of speaking are deluded, since there are no practical necessities and everything is possible, for us to accept, reject, or avoid.

Put like this, however, existentialism seems to be flatly false. It is not possible at every moment to choose any course of action, if only because previous decisions may themselves have limited our present choices. If I eat my cake now, I am not free to have it later on. Nor is it only my decisions that limit my freedom of choice. The decisions of others may do so as well. I may not be free to buy the stereo system I want because you have just bought the last one in stock.

It might be replied that these sorts of examples do not count against the general thesis of radical freedom because they are instances of logical impossibility—it is logic that determines that I cannot buy what is not for sale, and cannot eat what is already eaten. This says nothing more than that those courses of action that are not open to me are not open to me, a trivial truth of no interest. It places no restrictions upon my choice amongst those courses of action that *are* open to me. Within the boundaries of the logically possible, I am still inescapably free.

However, even this amended version of the thesis also seems to be false. In Canada (apart from Quebec) I am not free to buy a bottle of whisky anywhere except at a government liquor store. Here is a restriction on my freedom that is not a matter of logic but of law. An existentialist might reply that I am free to choose to break the law. This is true, but not enough to show that I am wholly free. Let us leave aside the important fact that this requires others to be willing to break the law also (I cannot sell liquor to myself). In saying that Canadians are not free to buy and sell each other liquor, I am of course speaking of legal freedom, and not of logical freedom. So though it is true that there is no *logical* bar to my buying liquor elsewhere, this does not show that I am free in the relevant sense. We can still distinguish between those logical possibilities that are legal possibilities and those that are not. It might be tempting to reply that, since the law can be broken, legal restraints are not restrictions on freedom properly so called. But this seems mistaken. A country in which I am legally free to speak out against the government is a freer country than one in which I am not, in a very straightforward sense of 'free'.

The general conclusion to which this example points us is that talk of 'freedom' always needs some qualification. To be free is to be free with respect to something—logic or the law in the examples just given. But once we have seen this we can also see that there are a good many important ways in which we can and cannot be free. For instance, I can invest where I will, but some investments are illegal and others are foolish. If an adviser were to say, 'You can't invest in that!', only on one possible interpretation would he mean that such an investment is logically impossible (the company in question no longer exists). It is just as likely for him to mean that it is financially impossible (the funds are not available) or that the proposed investment is illegal (you can't invest in cocaine) or that it is foolish (there are shares in many far more profitable firms available). Or (more rarely, perhaps) he might mean that it is unethical or immoral, that a morally decent investor cannot invest in it.

All these reasons present the investor with constraints upon what he can and cannot do. They rule out actions on the grounds that they are (respectively) logically impossible, financially impossible, illegal, imprudent, or immoral. An existentialist might continue to insist, as in the Canadian liquor example, that it is only the first two of these that present real restrictions on freedom, since it is possible to act illegally, imprudently, and immorally. For this reason, only the first two can be said to be constraints on our freedom. This is a thought that many people find compelling. What is logically or physically impossible does indeed seem to be impossible in a stronger sense than those things said to be legally or morally 'impossible'. But the important thing to observe is that logical and physical impossibilities are no more important than legal ones *from the point of view of practical deliberation.*

When we reason about what to do, we seek to restrict our choice of action; this is the point of the reasoning. We want to *rule out* certain courses of action. Of course, in order to be able to rule them out, we have to be able to consider them in the first place, so there must be a sense in which they are available to us. But in deciding against them on certain grounds, we are also acknowledging that there is reason to rule them out. The existentialist insists that all this 'ruling out' on legal, moral, or prudential grounds cannot make the action impossible, and hence cannot eliminate our freedom to choose it. Sartre says that we are condemned to be free, because in the absence of God "it is nowhere written that 'the good' exists, that one must be honest or must not lie, since we are now upon the plane where there are only men" (*Existentialism and Humanism*, p. 33). But this is just to confuse freedom from one point of view with freedom from every point of view. To be free of a divinely created natural law is not thereby to be free of every constraint or restriction.

If this is correct, the radical freedom of which existentialism speaks is at best a mere logical freedom. Within the boundaries of logical possibility, there are many other ways in which freedom of action may be constrained. But more than this. These additional constraints are not to be rejected but welcomed, since the freedom we ought to want is not unconstrained possibility of choice but *rational* freedom. To see what this means, consider the following example.

Suppose I am engaged in a piece of historical investigation, or am trying to arrive at a scientifically adequate explanation of some disease. In each case, freedom is essential; I want to be able to arrive freely at the right answer. That is to say, I must avoid formulating my answer in accordance with what would please my professors, my political masters, or those who supply funds for my work, or in accordance with what would be fashionable and attract headlines. The only thing that matters is that I arrive at the right answer by the free process of rational thought. But to say that I must be free to arrive at my own answer is not to say that I am free to arrive at just any answer. Some answers will be ignorant and silly, however appealing they might be to my imagination, and worthless from the point of view of the study in question. Of course, I am free to arrive at one of these worthless answers, in the sense that it is always possible for me to ignore the principles of good reasoning and falsify the evidence. But this freedom is not what we have in mind when we speak of freedom of thought. Conversely, when I am free of external pressure the fact that I arrive at the truth by obeying the rules of argument and evidence, is no restriction on my freedom. The freedom I want and that is worth having is not any less valuable because it is bound by rationality.

What the example shows is that some constraints, far from being restrictions on freedom, are just what make freedom valuable. When I check my calculations and say, 'That answer *can't* be right', I am freely engaged in thought about necessity. It is of no consequence to be told that I am free (which in an uninteresting sense I am) to accept any answer I like. The same point may be applied to other kinds of freedom. We have seen that trying to arrive at the truth in mathematics, science, or history does not represent any illegitimate constraint on human freedom, but on the contrary allows human beings to engage in the sort of freedom that is valuable, namely, rational freedom. Similarly to be free to choose your own values does not preclude an attempt to discover what is objectively good and evil. If in so doing we do discover the truth, this will no more be a fundamental rejection of freedom than the mathematician's pursuit of his subject.

This conclusion has important consequences for existentialist ways of thinking. To appreciate their full force, we need to see them in the context of a general review of the argument.

RESUMÉ

Existentialists hold that we are radically free with respect to our choice of values and style of life. In some deep sense, we define ourselves and what we stand for. One consequence of this radical freedom is that individuals have to accept full responsibility for what they do and are and believe. There is no God or external standard of 'the Good' to refer to, and no sociological or psychological conditioning to blame. This condition of radical freedom, however, is not one that everyone welcomes. Indeed, for many it is a cause of anguish and there is a strong inclination to hide from it by disguising the origin and manner of human choice. In other words, it is common and easy to act in bad faith, and a real achievement to act in good faith. Moreover, since even our choice of fundamental values is radically free, whether we act in good or bad faith is the supreme test of our human worth and dignity, and this is true regardless of the values we choose and act upon.

At this point, critics appeal to the case of the sincere Nazi. Doesn't existentialism oblige us to say that sincere Nazis were, at the very least, better than those who didn't really believe in the myth of the Aryan race and the desirability of the Holocaust? If so, it conflicts with a view at least as intelligible, namely, that the clear-sighted endorsement of evil is worse, not better, than shamefaced duplicity.

Such an objection, of course, amounts to simple counterassertion, but it is counterassertion that existentialism needs reason to rebut. In pursuit of such a reason, we explored a more radical line of thought, namely, that the sincere clear-sighted individual is the *source* of value. Hence, there is nothing further by which his choices may be judged good or evil. Here closer investigation showed that it is hard to see how value and meaning could be bestowed by individual acts of will. To say that individuals are free to choose their own values can at most mean that they are free to choose between pre-existent values.

Even this choice cannot be said to be radically free in the sense that existentialists have intended. The last section showed that there is no conflict between the idea of freedom and obedience to restrictions and constraints of certain kinds. Thought is not any the less free because it obeys the laws of logic. Similarly, our choice of values is not any the less free because it seeks to follow the truth about good and evil. What this shows is that subjective values can be objectively guided without any loss of freedom, and the pursuit of objectively rational values by which our lives and actions might be determined need not be an exercise in bad faith.

Of course, to say that the free pursuit of rational values is possible is not to give any guarantee of its success. Many philosophers, however, from Plato onwards, have approached the task with considerable optimism. The philosopher who held out the greatest hope for a rational investigation into the good life was the German eighteenth-century philosopher Immanuel Kant. His ideas are the subject of the next chapter.

SUGGESTED FURTHER READING

Original Sources
Soren Kierkegaard, *Concluding Unscientific Postscript*
Jean Paul Sartre, *Existentialism and Humanism*

Commentary
Patrick Gardiner, *Kierkegaard*
Frederick Sontag, *A Kierkegaard Workbook*
Anthony Manser, *Sartre*
John MacQuarric, *Existentialism*

Contemporary Discussion
D Z Phillips, 'Bad Faith and Sartre's Waiter', *Philosophy* 1981
R Campbell and D Collinson, *Ending Lives*, chaps. 4 and 5

CHAPTER FOUR

THE MORAL LIFE I: DUTY FOR DUTY'S SAKE

VIRTUE AND HAPPINESS: FARING WELL AND DOING RIGHT

Throughout the discussion so far, we have been thinking of the idea of the good life as the life it would be most desirable for a human being to lead. But it is time now to consider an important distinction that may be made between two senses of the expression 'the good life'. In one sense, 'the good life' means the most desirable or happiest life. In another, it means the worthiest or most virtuous human life.

This is a distinction that plays no significant part in Greek philosophical thinking. It first came to real prominence in eighteenth-century Europe. Although it is only then that we can see the distinction self-consciously drawn, it is arguable that its origin is to be found much earlier, with the emergence of Christianity. For one of the innovations of the Christian religion is the idea that the poor and the meek can be blessed, and, conversely, that even gaining possession of the whole world is not really profitable if we lose our souls in the process. As we shall see in a later chapter, these Christian ideas if they are to be discussed properly have to be examined within the larger context of *religious* conceptions of the good life. But there can be little doubt that they have had a large part to play in the formation of common moral ideas and in particular the widespread acceptance of the distinction we are concerned with in this chapter.

This distinction may be marked in a number of ways. One way is to contrast 'faring well' with 'doing right'. It is a commonplace that life can reward the most unprincipled men and women with material and social success. Indeed, since at least the days of the Hebrew psalmists people have been perplexed by the fact that it is often the wicked who prosper and that conversely the good not infrequently die young. Indeed, in general, life punishes the virtuous at least as often as it rewards them. And bitter experience has led people to the conclusion that there are occasions and contexts when prosperity is impossible for those who are virtuous.

One way of putting this observation from experience is to say that those who *do right* do not always *fare well*, while those who fare well do not always live as they should. Of course, the ancient Greek thinkers, though they did not formulate this distinction expressly, were aware of these familiar facts about happiness and virtue. In much of the philosophical writing that survives from that period, we can see attempts to accommodate them. Aristotle, it is true, is quite uncompromising in his belief that to be deprived of the social and material benefits of this life is to be deprived of a good life. But Plato sometimes advances the idea that such benefits are not the benefits that matter. In fact, we can see this idea at work in some of the arguments we have considered already. When Socrates argues with Thrasymachus and Callicles, he several times suggests that those who get their own way and triumph over others only *seem* to get the best of it. In reality, he claims, they do almost irreparable damage to their own most fundamental interests— the good of their own souls. Accordingly, Socrates argues that, faced with a choice between doing and suffering evil, those most interested in their own true welfare will choose to suffer rather than to commit evil.

The same line of thought appears in the New Testament. "What shall it profit a man", Jesus asks, "if he gain the whole world and lose his own soul?" Often this utterance is used by Christians for purely rhetorical purposes. It is offered not as a challenging thesis so much as a reminder of something we all know, namely, that "man does not live by bread alone", to use another biblical saying. But we lose the force of what Jesus is saying if we regard it merely as a pious sentiment that everyone in their less worldly moments will agree with. What we need to ask is just what contrast is at work in the question and · just what is meant by 'the soul' here.

This is specially important because for many people (even if it is not always thought nice to admit it) the answer to the New Testament question is obvious: 'His profit is the whole world, and how much more could he want?' It is this response and its implications that are explored in the famous story of Dr Faust, the man who gave his soul to Satan in return for unlimited material wealth and power.

The story of Dr Faust is based, probably, on a real sixteenth-century German magician, Johannes Faust. However, the legend that grew up about this man is much more important than the man himself. According to the legend, Faust entered into a pact with the devil, who promised, in return for his soul at death, to give him knowledge and magical power far surpassing that which human beings can normally attain and by which he might accomplish all his worldly desires. To ensure that both parts of the bargain are kept, Satan sends one of his more devious servants, Mephistopheles. It is he who conveys the knowledge and power and who is the instrument of Faust's death.

The original legend of Faust received much more sophisticated treatment at the hands of the English dramatist Christopher Marlowe in his famous play *The Tragical Life and Death of Dr Faust* and in the German poet Goethe's poem *Faust*. What is important about this story in all its versions is the distinction it forces us to make between the two senses of 'the good life'. If we are to find convincing reasons by which to persuade ourselves and others that Faust has the worst of the bargain, we cannot appeal to his failure to achieve the good things that life has to offer. That is precisely what Satan guaranteed to supply. So the good that he loses out on, and the evil he brings upon himself, must be of a quite different order.

There must be a difference in kind and not merely degree between the sorts of good and evil that are brought into question by the case of Faust. This means that we must elaborate a distinction between senses of the expression 'a good life'.

In doing this, we might appeal to the rewards and punishments of an afterlife, as generations of human beings have done. Indeed, the story itself encourages us to do this. Such an appeal raises two distinct questions. First, is there an afterlife? And second, if there is, do its rewards and punishments outweigh everything in this life? Both of these topics will be left to the last chapter, though here we might observe that it is the second question that is the more important for a philosophy of the good life. For the moment, if we stick to this world, and if we construe Faust's loss as contemporaneous rather than in the future, we need to show, first, that the *materially* best life (which he undoubtedly enjoys) is not the *morally* best life, and, second, that there is more to commend morality.

In other words, any adequate reply to the challenge represented by the story of Faust that aims to show that Faust makes a mistake must draw upon the distinction between *material* and *moral* goodness, between how we *fare* and how we *behave*, between *having* a good life and *leading* a good life. We should notice, however, that it is not enough to respond to Faust and those who think like him merely by drawing the distinction. We also have to show why one sort of good life— doing right—is preferable to the other—faring well. This means, as Plato saw, showing why, faced with the choice, we should prefer to suffer materially rather than do evil.

KANT AND 'THE GOOD WILL'

This is in fact the task that the eighteenth-century German philosopher Immanuel Kant set for himself. Kant was one of the greatest moral philosophers of all time. He developed and refined the very idea of 'the moral life' precisely to provide rational answers to these problems. Kant's most celebrated work in moral philosophy is entitled *Foundations of the Meta-physics of Morals*. As this title suggests, Kant aims to lay out the fundamental, rational character of moral thought and action. He begins the book with an argument similar to that we found Socrates using against Callicles, the argument that material benefits and personal talents may be used well or badly and hence cannot constitute the fundamental principle of good and evil. He writes:

Nothing in the world—indeed nothing even beyond the world—can possibly be conceived which could be called good without qualification except a good will. Intelligence, wit, judgement, and the other talents of the mind, however they may be named, or courage, resoluteness, and perseverance as qualities of temperament, are doubtless in many respects good and desirable. But they can become extremely bad and harmful if the will, which is to make use of these gifts of nature and which in its special constitution is called character, is not good. Power, riches, honour, even health, general well-being, and the contentment with one's condition which is called happiness, make for pride and even arrogance if there is not a good will to correct their influence on the mind and on its principles of action so as to make it universally conformable to its end. It need hardly be mentioned that the sight of a being adorned with no feature of a pure and good will, yet enjoying uninterrupted prosperity [i.e., anyone like Faust] can never give pleasure to a rational impartial observer. Thus the good will seems to constitute the indispensable condition even of worthiness to be happy. (p.9)

Kant's point is this: however wealthy or talented we may be, such benefits can be abused. Great wealth can be deliberately squandered on useless trivia, or used to corrupt and belittle others. Criminals and terrorists sometimes show great talent at electronics, mechanical invention, or strategic planning. Kant sees that, unless we are prepared to say that even in this sort of case these good things are *unqualifiedly* good, we must look elsewhere for the most basic standard of good and bad, right and wrong.

If material goods and natural talents cannot be the fundamental standard, what can it be? The examples just given of the abuse of good things might incline us to think that what is important is the purpose to which wealth and talent are put. But according to Kant this cannot be so because, however carefully we plan our actions, it is impossible to guarantee their outcome. (The Scottish poet Robert Burns expresses the same thought in a famous line, "The best laid schemes of mice and men, gang aft agley", i.e., go oft astray.) If, Kant says, we have a good will or intention in what we try to do, but "by a particularly unfortunate fate or the niggardly provision of a step-motherly nature" we are unable to accomplish the end in view, the good will that we had would still "sparkle as a jewel in its own right, as something that had full worth in itself".

An example may serve to make Kant's point a little clearer. Suppose someone works for an international charity, collecting money and organizing supplies of medicines for refugee camps. In the wake of a great disaster, she makes a Herculean effort and manages to fund and to dispatch a massive quantity of much needed medicine. But through no fault of hers, the storage facilities fail and the medicines become contaminated. Unfortunately, they are nonetheless administered in ignorance of their condition, and the result is that the death rate in the camps rises to a far higher level than if no medicines at all had been sent. This is, of course, a great tragedy. But even should the charity worker *feel* responsible, the real fault must be laid at the door of "a particularly unfortunate fate or the niggardly provision of a step-motherly nature", and her efforts towards an end that failed to materialize will still "sparkle as a jewel . . . that had full worth in itself".

Kant would make the same point with respect to the reverse kind of case. Suppose I see someone I regard as my enemy crossing a lonely road on a wild night when I am driving home, and try to run him down. As luck would have it, the sound of my sudden acceleration alerts him to a falling tree and he leaps into the ditch just in time to avoid being crushed beneath it.

By this curious route, my evil intention has saved his life. Nevertheless, this happy outcome seems to remove none of the wickedness of my action.

Intention and outcome, then, need to be separated, and it does not seem to be successful action that matters ultimately. This is because, in the first example, the unfortunate consequences did nothing to sully the fine nature of the intention, and, in the second example, the beneficial results did nothing to alter its evil character. Thus it seems to be the intention behind an action (what Kant calls "will"), rather than the success or failure of that action, that is all important.

About intention and will, however, more needs to be said, because intentions can themselves have differing motives behind them. The charity worker whose case was considered a moment ago can fail to bring about her good intentions and remain (so to speak) morally unscathed. But if we were to discover that her reason for attempting the relief work in the first place had nothing to do with the welfare of those involved but was rather a way of trying to win personal fame and glory, this would seriously undermine the moral merit in what she was doing. The same point is illustrated by the real case of bounty hunters in the American Wild West. These were people who aimed to do a good thing—bring criminals to justice. But often they themselves cared nothing for justice. They did what they did partly for monetary reward and partly because they enjoyed hunting down human beings. Such motives, on Kant's and on most people's view, completely destroy the moral worth of their actions.

But much more contentiously Kant also thinks that motivations of which we approve do not themselves carry moral worth. He says:

there are . . . many persons so sympathetically constituted that without any motive of vanity or selfishness they find an inner satisfaction in spreading joy, and rejoice in the contentment of others which they have made possible. But I say that, however dutiful and aimiable it may be, that kind of action has no true moral worth. (*Foundations of the Metaphysics of Morals*, p. 14)

This is because it arises from inclination. Kant does not think, as some people have supposed him to, that you ought never to enjoy doing good. He does think, however, that there is an important difference between the actions of someone who spontaneously and with pleasure does what is right and the same actions on the part of someone who performs them, with difficulty perhaps, *but solely because it is right.* Kant invites us to consider the case of someone whose life has been easy and happy and who takes a great interest in others and attends to the needs of those in distress. Suddenly his life is clouded by some great personal sorrow. He finds that he can take no interest in the affairs of other people and is constantly overwhelmed by self-concern, though he still has the means to alleviate distress and the need to do so is as strong as ever.

Now suppose him to tear himself, unsolicited by inclination, out of this dead insensibility and to perform this action only from duty and without any inclination—then for the first time his action has genuine moral worth. (*Foundations of the Metaphysics of Morals*, p. 14)

The reason Kant thinks that true moral merit or demerit attaches to actions regardless of the feelings of those who perform them lies in his belief that "inclination cannot be commanded" whereas action can. Since people can only be praised or blamed where they can be held responsible, praise and blame can only attach to action, not to feelings. You cannot make yourself glad to see someone, but you can nonetheless be welcoming. You cannot help finding pleasure in the failures of people you dislike, but you can, despite your feelings, act in a kindly way towards them. It follows, on Kant's view, that it is action not feeling that determines moral worth.

But recall the earlier examples and argument. We must

combine this conclusion with the claim that success is not morally important either. What matters fundamentally is that someone should aim to do what is right because it is right. Whether or not his natural inclinations support or oppose this, and whether his good intention comes off or not are both irrelevant, the first because we cannot command our feelings and the second because we cannot completely control the world about us. The only thing wholly within our control, and hence the only thing for which we can be praised or blamed from a moral point of view, is the will. This is why Kant says that it is only a good will that can be unqualifiedly good, and that the unqualifiedly good will is doing your duty for duty's sake.

Let us, for the moment at any rate, agree with this. We are left with an important question. If the only unqualifiedly good thing is a good will, and if the good will is not good because of what it results in, how are we to determine or demonstrate its goodness? In what does its goodness consist? Kant's answer is that the good will is a purely rational will. To see what he means by this, however, needs a good deal of explanation.

DAVID HUME AND PRACTICAL REASON

Philosophers have often elaborated a distinction between theoretical reason and practical reason. The distinction they have in mind is that between reasoning which is directed at telling you what to *think* or *believe*, and reasoning that is directed at telling you what to *do*. In fact, however, the distinction is rather hard to draw; even the way I have just put it is open to objection since it is quite correct to speak of beliefs about what to do. But that there is some difference or other is fairly plain, because generally speaking a piece of theoretical reason, by which we mean appeal to evidence and argument, ends with a conclusion about what is the case—for example, 'Smoking is a contributory cause of lung diseases'. Practical reason, on the other hand, which also consists in a review of evidence and arguments, ends with a conclusion about what ought to be done—for example, 'You ought to take a course in accountancy before you leave college'.

Some philosophers have thought that the difference between theoretical and practical reason is this: practical reason requires some *desire* or other on the part of the reasoner before the reasoning has any force. To see why they have thought this, we need only take the example offered a moment ago. Imagine an argument designed to convince you that you should take a course in accountancy before you leave college. It might run like this:

The best paid jobs for graduates at the present time are to be found in the financial and commercial sectors. Employers don't want to recruit people who think they already know all about business. But at the same time, they want people who are not totally unfamiliar with business practice, and who can show that the intellectual abilities they have in history or philosophy will show themselves in ways beneficial to the company. So to have a course or two in accountancy is to make yourself a more attractive prospect in the job market than either a business graduate or a pure arts graduate.

As an argument, this has no doubt proved persuasive to many, but it is obvious that its strength is a function of two things. First, the facts it alleges about jobs in the finance sector and about company recruiters must be true. Second, the person addressed must *want* a well-paid job. If either of these conditions does not hold, the argument loses its force. So, for instance, if the person I am speaking to has a private income and is thus not in search of a job at all, the conclusion 'You ought to take a course in accounting' doesn't apply.

In this respect, the second example differs markedly from the first. If evidence and argument are mounted that show that smoking contributes to lung disease, only the facts alleged need be true for the conclusion to follow and for me to be obliged to accept it. What I want or do not want does not come into the matter. Of course, people sometimes allow their desires to blind them to the truth, but the point is that when this happens their belief is irrational, contrary to reason. In the case of practical reason, on the other hand, your desire determines the applicability of the argument.

One way of putting this is to say that practical reason is *hypothetical*. That is, it takes the form '*If* you want such and such, *then* you ought to do so and so'. If, on the other hand, you *don't* want such and such, nothing follows about what you ought to do. This means that practical reason, at least so far as the example we have been discussing goes, is not a very forceful guide to conduct, since we can escape its demands by abandoning or modifying our desires.

Some philosophers have in fact claimed that all practical reason is hypothetical and dependent upon desire in this way. The Scottish philosopher David Hume, who was mentioned briefly in Chapter One, held this view. In a famous passage of his *A Treatise of Human Nature*, he claims, "Reason is, and ought only to be the slave of the passions, and can never pretend to any other office than to serve and obey them" (p. 415). By this he means that the use of reason can only be practical in so far as it points the means to ends that we independently desire.

This view of Hume's has what some people regard as a curious consequence, namely, that we cannot reason about desires and cannot therefore declare any desire to be irrational. Hume in fact accepts this.

'Tis not contrary to reason (he says) to prefer the destruction of the whole world to the scratching of my finger. 'Tis not contrary to reason for me to chuse my total ruin, to prevent the least uneasiness of an *Indian* or person wholly unknown to me. 'Tis as little contrary to reason to prefer even my own acknowledg'd lesser good to my greater, and have a more ardent affection for the former than the latter. (*A Treatise of Human Nature*, p. 416)

We need to be very clear about what Hume is saying here. He is not commending any of the attitudes which he describes. All three are abnormal, and may even be said to be unreasonable, if by reasonable we just mean 'what ordinary people would accept as sensible'. No doubt if we were to come across someone who thought so much of himself that he really did express a preference to see the whole world destroyed rather than have a scratch on his little finger, we would be appalled at his attitude. Similarly, anyone who sincerely preferred to go through agonies rather than have someone quite unknown to him suffer the mildest discomfort would no doubt be treated as odd to the point of madness. And those who are self-destructive, that is, those who seem positively to seek the things that harm them and belittle what is in their best interests are generally recognized as psychologically problematic. But none of these attitudes, according to Hume, is strictly irrational, since no intellectual error of any kind is being made. There is no fact of the matter, or mathematical-type calculation, or logically provable inference about which the person in question is mistaken. The difference between normality and abnormality lies entirely in the uncommon character of the *desires* these people have.

If this is true, it is clear that no appeal to reason could produce a conclusive ground for action because all such appeals come into play only in a subservient role to desire, and consequently Reason in the abstract is silent upon practical matters. This means that general principles such as 'You ought not to murder' must sooner or later depend upon some desire or other, the desire not to rob others of their most valued possession for instance, or the desire not to cause anguish and suffering to friends and relatives. But what if someone does not have these desires? What if they care nothing? Does this mean that the principle does not apply to them? And is there here the further implication that the principle would cease to apply to me, if only I could bring myself to a state of mind in which I, too, no longer cared about the lives and feelings of others?

On the face of it, this seems quite unacceptable. Most people would say of those who are callously indifferent to the feelings of others not that they are free from obligations because they don't care, but that they ought to care. But if Hume is right, there is no further rational basis upon which this 'ought' is to be based. They don't care and " 'tis not contrary to reason" that they do not. If Hume is right, how could feelings and desires be made subject to reason? You either have them or you don't.

HYPOTHETICAL AND CATEGORICAL IMPERATIVES

It was this question of practical rationality that caused Kant to try to provide an alternative account of practical reason to Hume's, although he does not expressly discuss Hume in the *Foundations*. If we think of the conclusions of practical reason as *imperatives* (directives about what to do), these come, Kant argues, not in a single type, but in two different types. There are first of all those that Hume rightly identifies as hypothetical, that is, imperatives the force of which relies on having the appropriate desire. This can be seen from the following imaginary dialogue.

'If you want to lose weight, you ought to give up ice-cream' (hypothetical imperative).
'But I don't want to lose weight'.
'Well, in that case, you've no reason to give up ice-cream'.

Hypothetical imperatives themselves fall into two kinds. Kant calls recommendations of the sort just given *technical* imperatives because they are concerned with the technical means to chosen ends. Then there are *assertoric* imperatives. These imperatives also rest upon a desire, not a desire that someone happens to have, however, but a desire that human beings tend naturally to share, and which in consequence is not usually expressly referred to. In the normal run of things, these carry more force, but not necessarily so.

'You ought to give up drugs because they're ruining your health' (assertoric imperative).
To this someone *could* reply, 'I *want* to ruin my health'.
In which case, we could only reply, 'You're crazy to my mind, but if that's what you want go right ahead'.

In cases like this, the value we had reasonably supposed to be common to us is not in fact shared, and the recommendation to action fails to apply just as much as in the case of a technical imperative.

In contrast to both kinds of hypothetical, there are *categorical* imperatives. These have the very special property of resting upon no hypothetical condition whatever, and hence cannot be rejected by denying any conditional desire. It is imperatives of this sort that are supposed to block the move that Hume's account of practical reason leaves open.

'It's your duty not to cheat others, because it leads to their hurt and unhappiness' (assertoric imperative).
'But I don't want to do my duty'.
'Well you *ought* to do your duty' (categorical imperative).

With the discovery of categorical imperatives, Kant thought, we have reached the heart of morality. Categorical imperatives transcend our wants and desires by presenting us with rational principles of action in the light of which those desires themselves are to be assessed. Philosophers usually express this by saying that such principles of conduct are *overriding*, that is, they take precedence over other sorts of considerations when we are deciding what to do.

In fact, this idea of overriding principles of conduct fits rather well with a view that many people have about morality,

namely, that it is a more important dimension to human behaviour than any other. If we show that some proposal is likely
to be unprofitable, or unpopular, we are providing reasons
against it, but not overriding reasons. For considerations of
profit and mere popularity (or so it is commonly thought)
should not take precedence over what is morally required of
us. The profit motive is a rational one to have, but it must take
second place to honesty. Making people laugh is a good thing,
but not when it involves telling slanderous lies about others.
In short, moral uprightness requires us to give second place to
fears and favours. This common belief about the overriding
character of moral considerations is what makes Kant's talk of
categorical imperatives appealing. Or at least it does if there
are such things. So far, in fact, we have simply had drawn for
us a contrast between two basic types of imperative (the technical and the assertoric are fundamentally the same). We have
no clear indication as to how categorical imperatives are
grounded in reason.

And there is a real difficulty about this just because it is
easy to see that hypothetical imperatives are grounded in reason precisely in virtue of their being hypothetical. 'If you want
credit for this course, you must pass the exam'. If you *do* want
credit, you can test the rational basis of the recommendation
by checking the rules to see if it is *true* that credit is obtainable
only by passing the exam. The rationality of the recommendation is simply a function of its truth. Or, again, 'If you want
clear skin, you ought to use perfume-free soap'. If you *do* want
clear skin, it is open to you to test the truth of this recommendation by examining the effects of soap with and without
perfume.

But in the case of a categorical imperative, there does not
seem to be any truth to check. 'You ought not to steal, if you
don't want to end up in jail' can be checked by looking into
facts about detection and conviction rates. But what facts can
we look into to check the categorical 'You ought not to steal'?

PURE PRACTICAL REASON AND THE MORAL LAW

Sometimes it has been suggested that there is a special order of moral 'facts' that are relevant here, and that we can check by using a special faculty, our moral sense or our conscience. This idea brings with it a number of very great problems—how are we to decide between competing imperatives that are both said to arise from conscience, for instance? These are not problems we need to deal with here, however, for Kant's approach is somewhat different. He thinks that we can check the rationality of categorical imperatives by examining them in the light of what he calls pure practical reason. Kant calls it *pure* practical reason because on his view it involves no appeal to matters of empirical fact or sensory experience but to principles of intellectual reasoning alone. To see how it works, he invites us to take part in a thought experiment.

Imagine a world of perfectly rational beings. (Let us call them angels though this is not Kant's terminology.) To say that such beings are perfectly rational is to say that they always *do* what we, being less than perfect, always *ought* to do. Kant expresses this by saying that what is objective law for angels (demonstrably the right thing to do) is also subjectively necessary for them (just what by nature angels are inclined to do). This is not true for us. What is objectively right is usually experienced by us as a *constraint* on action, something we *ought* to do, because our natural inclinations often lie in other directions. By contrast, for a perfectly rational creature there is no sense of constraint, no sense of being bound or required, and from this we can see that in a world of angels the laws of rationality would be like the laws of nature are in this one. We could explain and predict the behaviour of the angels by appealing to moral laws, laws of right and wrong, just in the way that we can explain and predict the behaviour of liquids, gases, and solids by appealing to the laws of physics. Angels do what is morally right as automatically as water runs downhill.

Now this supplies us, in fact, with a way of determining what the moral law is. Suppose I propose to perform an action for a reason (what Kant calls a maxim). I can now ask myself, 'Could acting on that maxim be a law of nature in a world of perfect beings?' If it could not, I have shown that the proposed action is not in accordance with pure practical reason and therefore not morally right. Consequently, it is contrary to a rational will to perform the proposed action for the reason given.

This is a formal statement of the principle, of course, abstracted from any particular case. Kant offers us four examples of the detailed application of his method of pure practical reason.

1. A man who has suffered a great deal, and anticipates even more suffering before his life is over, wonders whether it would not be better if he took his own life. But he asks himself what his reason would be, and whether he could consistently will that people always act on the reason. His reason is that life holds out a greater likelihood of bad than good for him, and so the maxim under examination is: 'Whenever the future seems bad rather than good, kill yourself'. But immediately he sees (Kant argues) that this could not be a law of nature because it is precisely the fact of the future's looking gloomy that provides us with a reason to work for its improvement. A world in which the would-be suicide's maxim held as a law of nature would pretty soon destroy itself because everything that supplies good reason to work for the continuation of life would lead people to kill themselves. From this it follows, Kant thinks, that suicide is against the moral law.

2. A man is in debt. He has the opportunity to borrow money with a promise to repay, but he knows that in fact he will never be able to repay it. He is nonetheless tempted to make the promise, a lying promise, but asks himself whether this would be morally right. Once again, the categorical imperative is appealed to, and he sees that, were it to be a law of nature that those in dire financial circumstances always made

lying promises, this would lead immediately to the collapse of the institution of promising since lenders would know that the money would not be repaid and would refuse to lend. It follows that lying promises are contrary to the moral law.

3. A man has a natural talent for something, but an inclination to idleness tempts him to ignore and fail to improve it. He asks himself whether there is anything morally wrong in this. And immediately he sees, or so Kant claims, that though a world of essentially idle and pleasure-seeking people is possible, it is impossible to will that such a world exist, since any rational creature will want to keep open the opportunities that different kinds of talent provide.

4. A prosperous man sees many others around him in poverty and hardship but says, "What concern is that of mine? I have no desire to contribute to the welfare of the needy. And, should I fall on hard times, I have no intention of calling upon others myself". It is possible, Kant says, to imagine a world in which everyone takes that attitude, but it is impossible to will, through your will, that such a world come into existence. For then you would have robbed yourself of the help and sympathy of others, which you are likely to want when times get hard.

These examples are meant only as illustrations of a general thesis about morality, and it is to that thesis we must return. But it is worth remarking that Kant's attempt to apply pure practical reason to particular examples is a marked failure. None of these examples is convincing. Take the last. It depends upon the hard-hearted man wanting precisely what he says he does not mean to claim—the help of others should he himself fall upon hard times. It is certainly open to Kant to doubt that anyone would continue to hold this view once hard times were actually upon him. But if so, this is a result of his human nature, which Kant thinks has no part in pure practical reason, and does not show that the principle "Offer and ask no help" *cannot* be consistently maintained, even if, *as a matter of fact*, it is not likely to be consistently maintained by those who hold it.

Or consider the first example. This is supposed to show that suicide is out. But it does nothing of the kind. We can consistently maintain that it is rational to commit suicide when circumstances are *very* adverse without thereby agreeing that suicide is justified in the face of *any adversity whatever*. But it is only by equating the two that Kant's conclusion follows.

UNIVERSALIZABILITY

Still, if Kant does the job of illustration badly, this does not necessarily mean that the basic philosophy at work is unsound. What is important is whether the method he proposes for deciding what morality requires of us is satisfactory. That method consists in applying a test to every reasoned action, a test that has subsequently become known in moral philosophy as 'universalizability'. This is the procedure of seeing whether your own reasons for action could apply to everyone equally or whether they amount to nothing better than special pleading in your own case.

There are many sophisticated twists and turns that can be given to the philosophical elaboration of this test, but in fact it is not far in spirit from what is a common enough way of thinking. When some action is proposed, people often ask of themselves and others, 'What if everyone did that?' This is thought to be an important objection, but it is open to two different interpretations. Sometimes the idea is that everyone's doing it would lead to a cumulatively undesirable result. For example, I might object to your walking on the grass on the grounds that if everyone did it there would soon be no lawn. Alternatively, the idea is that some actions are impossible for everyone, and hence involve special pleading on the part of the individual. For example, if I try to go out of turn instead of standing in line, the appeal to what everyone might do invokes the idea of destructive chaos. If everyone tries to go out of turn, the social order 'turns' and 'lines' created are undermined. It is in this second test of universalizability that Kant is interested, and he gives it its first formal elaboration. It is important to see, however, that he is not speculating upon what the general run of mankind would do, but rather what we could consistently will to be the behaviour of all mankind. We are not asking, 'What will everyone do?' but 'What if everyone were to do it?', knowing, of course, that everyone will not. The test is about consistency, not consequences.

We have considered a number of categorical imperatives—you ought not to murder, you ought not to make lying promises, you ought to develop such talents as you have, and so on—but Kant argues that these can all be derived from one basic imperative from which all the laws of moral conduct can be derived. It is this: "I should never act in such a way that I could not also will that my maxim should be universal law" (*Foundations of the Metaphysics of Morals*, p. 18). What he means is this. If you want to know whether what you propose to do is morally right or not, ask yourself whether you can consistently will that everyone, whenever they have the same reason as you do, should act in that way. Or, to put it in philosophers' jargon, ask yourself if you can consistently universalize the maxim of your action.

Kant goes on, with an ever-increasing degree of abstraction, to formulate two other versions of the categorical imperative. His argument is complex, and the resulting claim is that the fundamental moral law is one which requires from us 'respect for persons'. He formulates this version thus: "Act so that you treat humanity, whether in your own person or that of another always as an end and never as a means only" (*Foundations of the Metaphysics of Morals*, p. 47). This formulation has become known as the ideal of 'respect for persons'. It has been more influential in Western moral philosophy than perhaps any other ethical idea, and to understand it properly a great deal needs to be said about it. But it is not necessary here either to trace all the steps by which Kant reaches this ideal or to explore the ideal itself more closely. For what we want to know is not whether 'respect for persons' is a good moral principle, but whether the conception of the moral life in which it is one element is a conception that we have good reason to accept. And enough has been said about Kant's philosophy to allow us to summarize and examine this conception. First, the summary.

SUMMARY OF KANT'S PHILOSOPHY

When we ask questions about 'the good life', there is built into them an ambiguity. We can mean 'the happiest life' or we can mean 'the worthiest life'. It is the latter that is more important, since the best a human being can hope for is to be worthy of happiness, and to attain such worthiness is to lead a moral life. This does not consist in doing good, however, because whether the good we try to do actually comes about is not a matter over which, ultimately, we can exercise control. Between aspiration and reality, misfortune may well intervene. Neither does the moral life consist in having the right sort of mentality. Whether we are cheerful, friendly, generous, and optimistic, or solemn, withdrawn, thrifty, and pessimistic is a matter of the nature with which we are born, and hence also something over which we can exercise little control. Consequently, our temper, good or bad, is not something which can properly attract either praise or blame.

What *can* properly be examined from a moral point of view is our will, the intention behind the things we do and say, because this is wholly within our control as rational agents. Be we rich or poor, clever or stupid, handsome or ugly, jolly or sad, every one of us can aim to do what is right because it is right, and if we succeed in this we succeed in living a morally good life.

But how do we know what is right? We know it by considering what actions are categorically forbidden or required, not because of their consequences or outcome in any particular case, but on grounds of pure reason alone. These are all those actions that match up to the test of the most fundamental categorical imperative of universalizability and respect for persons.

IS THE KANTIAN MORAL LIFE A GOOD ONE?

Kant's moral philosophy has generated a huge quantity of comment, interpretation, and criticism. A great deal of this has served to show that there are complexities in his thought of which even he was not wholly aware. Moreover, however impressive his attempt to delineate a clear conception of morality pure and simple and to give it a firm foundation in reason, it is widely agreed that Kant's philosophy fails. Some of the reasons for this failure lie in quite technical philosophical issues which are difficult to explain briefly or simply. But the larger part of the failure arises from features of Kant's conception of the moral life whose unattractiveness or inadequacy can be shown without too much complexity. There are in fact three main objections. These have to do with the separation of intention and outcome, the test of universalizability, and the idea of doing one's duty for its own sake. We will consider each of these in turn.

ACT, INTENTION, AND OUTCOME

Kant holds that the moral worth of an action must reside in the will with which it is performed, or, as we would more naturally say, in the intention behind it. This is, as we have seen, because people cannot be held responsible for, nor can they claim the merit of, outcomes over which they have very imperfect control. It is both pointless and wrong to praise and blame people for things that they could neither prevent nor bring about. An "unfortunate fate" or a "step-motherly nature" may bring our best intentions to nothing. It is to our intentions, then, that praise and blame must be attached.

Many people have found this an intuitively appealing idea, and yet it is difficult to see that it can really be held. If we want to insist that moral merit and demerit attach to the intentions behind an action, it is hard to deny that actions and their consequences must also be taken into account. Intending to murder someone is wrong, presumably, because murder is wrong. If I am to murder someone, it is not enough for me to pull a trigger or plunge a knife. My victim must actually die as a consequence of what I do. Intending to save someone from drowning is meritorious, presumably, because the action of saving someone is. It is not enough for me to have reached for someone's hand, or pulled someone aboard; the person must go on living as a consequence. If, then, we are to concern ourselves with the moral character of intention, we are at the same time obliged to take actions into account and cannot take as indifferent an attitude to success as Kant's way of thinking would suggest.

Someone might deny this, deny in other words that actions are morally important. They might claim that what matters from a moral point of view is not what we *do* but what we *try* to do. This is in fact a common thought. Many people think that moral right and wrong is not about accomplishing things or being successful but about trying hard and doing your best. 'At least you tried' is often offered as moral compensation for failure.

But though the belief that trying is more important than succeeding is quite widely shared, at least one important objection can be brought against it. This objection arises from the fact noted before that attempts and intentions have to be expressed in actions. Trying to do something is not the same as doing it, but it is still the performance of some action. If this is true, it necessarily follows that the attribution of almost every *attempted* action also carries an implicit reference to actions and outcomes, since attempts are themselves actions.

To see this we need only consider once more the example of taking and saving life. I cannot be accused of trying to murder you unless I have succeeded in some action or other—holding up a gun, firing it, waving a knife, putting a poisonous substance in your food. If none of these actions or others like them take place, there is no substance to the claim that I tried to murder you. And this means that some consequential actions must take place if we are to talk even of the moral assessment of attempts.

Similarly, I cannot claim to have tried to save a drowning child unless I have succeeded in doing something else—reaching out my hand, running for a life belt, pulling at his body. Were you to see me sitting perfectly still and accuse me of callous indifference to his plight, it would hardly do for me to reply that I had tried to save him but that an "unfortunate fate" or a "step-motherly nature" had intervened in every one of my attempts and robbed my good intentions of any result whatsoever. I cannot reasonably say that I have attempted to do anything if none of my attempts have met with any success of any kind.

The upshot of this argument is really very simple. If we are to make a moral assessment of the lives of ourselves and others, we have to decide not only whether what we *meant to* do was right or wrong, but also whether what we *did* was right or wrong. Since doing anything at all involves having some effect on the world, however small, part of the assessment will be concerned with the success of our intentions. This means that success cannot be left out of the calculation in the way that Kant suggests. It is not enough, in short, simply to have a good will. A good will that accomplishes nothing whatever cannot "shine like a jewel".

UNIVERSALIZABILITY (MORE)

Of course, none of this shows that will and intention are not of great moral importance. Nor does it show that intentions do not matter. It is still the case that people who mean well, but whose good intentions do not come off for reasons quite independent of their actions, deserve moral commendation. From this it follows that at least some moral assessment is based upon considerations other than success.

It is here that Kant's most widely discussed contribution to moral philosophy comes into play, namely his formulations of the categorical imperative. Kant claims to offer us a test by which our actions and intentions can be assessed, a test quite independent of desired or actual outcomes. This is the test of universalizability. According to Kant, we have to ask ourselves whether an action we propose to perform could consistently be performed by everyone similarly placed and with the same reasons. And, he argues, such a test plainly rules out many of the sorts of actions the common morality of his day condemned—suicide, lying promises, failure to develop one's talents.

We saw, however, that Kant's own illustrations of this principle are far from convincing. The fact that they do not work very well is not in itself conclusive proof that the test is a poor one, because it might be made to work better than Kant himself manages to do. But when we try to apply it more rigorously, it turns out, in fact, that the test is too *easily* satisfied. This is illustrated most readily with another example.

In Chapter Three we saw that the ethics of authenticity, i.e., the view that good actions are made good by the sincerity with which they are performed, falls foul of 'the sincere Nazi'. This is the person who engages in conduct widely recognized to be evil, but who does so with enthusiastic sincerity. Common sense suggests that this sincerity, far from making those actions good or even better, makes them *worse*. Indeed, it is arguable that bad actions become truly evil when they are freely, deliberately, and sincerely performed.

A similar objection to the Kantian ethics of intention can be found in what we might call 'the *consistent* Nazi'. This is the person who acts on the maxim 'This person should be exterminated because he or she is a Jew'. Now according to Kant's moral philosophy we can put this maxim to the test by appealing to the categorical imperative: "Act only according to that maxim by which you can at the same time will that it should become a universal law." And we might point out to the Nazi that if it were a universal law of nature that Jews were regularly exterminated, then *he* would be exterminated if *he* were a Jew. If, given that in the actual case it was not unknown for enthusiastic Aryans to be found to have Jewish ancestry, the Nazi in question were to engage in some special pleading, some argument which made his own a special case, we could indeed accuse him of failing to judge in accordance with the categorical imperative.

But if he were a *consistent* Nazi, who not only conceded but positively endorsed the idea that were *he* to be found to be Jewish he, too, must perish, we could not find fault with him on these grounds. To be prepared to promote political ideas even if it puts you on the losing side may be an unlikely attitude of mind for most people, but it is certainly possible and displays consistency. However, if a policy of genocide is deeply mistaken from a moral and every other point of view, consistency in its application is hardly any improvement. And insofar as people are prepared to sacrifice *themselves* in a programme of genocide, this reveals not their moral rectitude but their fanaticism.

The same point can be made about one of Kant's own examples. Recall the man who prided himself on his independence and neither gave nor asked for charity. Kant says that such a man could hardly will that were he himself to fall on hard times it should nonetheless be a universal law of nature that no one assist him in his poverty. Now it may be *psychologically* unlikely that an individual in need could wish to receive no assistance (though surely we are familiar with people who are too proud to receive charity). But it is plainly not a *logical* contradiction. The opponents of charity can as easily apply their harsh doctrine to themselves as to others if they choose. Whilst we may remark upon their rather grim, almost inhuman, consistency, this does not make their action any better, because it does not make them any the less uncharitable.

Once more, consistency does not seem to bring objectionable actions any nearer to what we recognize as moral right and wrong.

The 'consistent Nazi' objection is not merely a matter of comparing the results of universalizability with common moral belief. It can also be used to show that the test of universalizability is quite powerless when it comes to deciding between competing moral recommendations. Consider two, contradictory, recommendations—'Never kill people just because they're Jewish' and 'Always kill people who are Jewish because they're Jewish'. The case of the consistent Nazi shows that the second of these recommendations, however loathsome, can be made to square with the demands of the categorical imperative, and it should be fairly obvious that the first can be made to satisfy it. But if contradictory proposals can both satisfy the test of universalizability, it follows that that test is unable to discriminate between good and bad recommendations. In short, it cannot tell us what to do. From this it follows that Kantian universalizability cannot provide the means to determine the good life.

DUTY FOR DUTY'S SAKE

So far we have seen that Kant's view of the good life as the moral life is marred in two respects. First, the emphasis he places upon moral goodness residing in our will or intention to do our duty and not in the good or bad consequences of our actions is mistaken, since a complete divorce between intention, action, and outcome is impossible. For this reason, there can be no question of judging an intention right or wrong without considering the goodness or badness of at least *some* of the consequences of those intentions. And this means that the moral quality of a life cannot be decided purely in terms of will and intention.

Second, even if we agree that intention must form a large part of our moral assessment, the idea of requiring the reasons upon which we act to be universally applicable, i.e., the requirement of universalizability, does not supply us with an effective test for deciding which intentions are good and which are bad. People can consistently pursue evil courses of action, and wholly contradictory recommendations can consistently be based upon the same reasoning. It follows that universalizability is not an effective test at all. Any action or mode of conduct can be made to meet it, and hence no course of action can be shown to be ruled out by it.

But besides these two objections there is a third. Kant observes, with some plausibility, that it is not enough to do one's duty. Morality requires that we do it because it is our duty and for no other reason. In other words, a morally good life does not consist merely in acting in accordance with moral right and wrong, but doing so *because of an express commitment* to moral right and wrong. Those who do not steal because they never have the chance or inclination to, or because they are fearful of punishment, are to be contrasted with those who never steal because it is wrong to steal. This is what is meant by saying that they do their duty for duty's sake. And, according to Kant, acting on this reason exceeds in value acting in the same way for any other reason. It is worth recalling the passage quoted earlier where Kant writes:

To be kind where one can is duty, and there are, moreover, many persons so sympathetically constituted that without any motive of vanity or selfishness they find an inner satisfaction in spreading joy, and rejoice in the contentment of others which they have made possible. But I say that, however dutiful and amiable it may be, that kind of action has no true moral worth. (*Foundations of the Metaphysics of Morals*, p. 14)

Let us for a moment agree with Kant. If the moral life is the life of duty for duty's sake, and the best (in the sense of finest) form of human life is the moral life, we are rather swiftly led to the somewhat unpalatable conclusion that many happy and attractive human lives fall far short of the most admirable kind of life, and may even realize nothing of it at all. Consider for instance someone who is talented and clever and who, being generously disposed to use these great gifts for the health and happiness of others, works hard on inventing and developing an ingenious device that is of great use to the physically handicapped. The work is enjoyable, though not specially well paid; much good is gladly done, but without any sense of 'doing one's duty'. Is it really plausible to claim that such a life is devoid of moral worth?

There is, however, an even more implausible and uncomfortable conclusion to be drawn from Kant's conception of morality, and that is that we must attribute high moral worth to deeply *unattractive* human lives, and hence prefer them to the sort of life just described. That this is an unpalatable consequence of the theory is brought out by the following description of one of Anthony Trollope's characters in *The Eustace Diamonds*, Lady Linlithgow.

In her way Lady Linlithgow was a very powerful human being. She knew nothing of fear, nothing of charity, nothing of mercy, and nothing of the softness of love. She had no imagination. She was worldly, covetous and not unfrequently cruel. But she meant to be true and honest, though she often failed in her meaning; and she had an idea of her duty in life. She was not self-indulgent. She was as hard as an oak post—but then she was also as trustworthy. No human being liked her;—but she had the good word of a great many human beings.

This rather appalling picture of rectitude that knows nothing of happiness but means to do its duty can hardly strike us as the model of the life we ought to lead. This is especially true when set beside that of happy hardworking lives in which a good deal of good is done but where duty for its own sake plays little or no part. Of course, the defender of Kant's moral philosophy might use the same argument that has been employed at several other places in this book—it is not a good reason to reject a philosophy of value just because it conflicts with what we commonly think; after all, what we commonly think about morality and the good life may be wrong, just as what people have thought about health and medicine has often been corrected by scientific investigation. Perhaps then Lady Linlithgow's life *is* to be admired as a good example of the sort of life we ought to lead.

But the conflict with common thought is not so easily ignored. Here we must return to the opening topic of this chapter, doing right and faring well. There we drew a distinction between two senses of the expression 'the good life'. In one it meant 'living as we ought', what we may call 'the virtuous life', and in the other 'living as we would like to', what we may call 'the happy life'. Just as in the story of Faust we find an attempt to abandon the constraints of virtue entirely in the exclusive pursuit of happiness, so in Kant's moral philosophy we find an attempt to divorce completely the concerns of virtue and happiness, in the belief that the most important thing is to lead a moral life. It is this attempt at a complete separation that makes possible the construction of lives and characters like Lady Linlithgow which, though naturally repellent, we must regard as exemplary instances of the Kantian good life.

But in fact virtue and happiness cannot be held completely apart in this way. This can be seen if we consider once more the foundations of Kant's thought. His concern is to urge upon us an ideal greater than that of the happy life, namely, a life *worthy* of happiness. There are two ways in which we might think of this as the greater ideal. On the one hand, we might suppose that though a happy life is good, a deservedly happy life is better. This is, I think, the other side to our thought about the wicked who prosper, that they don't *deserve* to prosper. On this way of thinking, the good life has two aspects, virtue *and* happiness.

Kant takes it another way. The moral life is a superior mode of life because so long as we are worthy to be happy, there is a sense in which we don't need happiness itself. We have attained the most admirable life. Virtue is its own reward. This is how it is possible for those who are unhappy and unattractive to lead good lives on the Kantian model. The question arises, however, concerning why anyone should aspire to such an existence. What, in other words, could motivate anyone to lead a moral life conceived of in this way?

To see how important this question is in the context, imagine a world in which "unfortunate fate" and "a step-motherly nature" constantly held the upper hand, so that to act in accordance with the moral law was a surefire way of courting disaster. (There have occasionally been societies in which this condition seems to have prevailed.) In such a world, virtue and happiness are not only separate but in constant competition, and people are regularly faced with the choice of doing their duty for its own sake at the cost of personal misery, or ignoring the call of duty and securing their own happiness and that of their families and friends. What should they do in such a world?

On the one side, there is plainly reason to forget about duty—it will lead to unhappiness. On the other side, if we ignore objections considered earlier and assume that Kant's arguments are sound, there is the conflict with *pure* practical reason. But what does this amount to in the end? That if I act against the moral law, I will be acting irrationally, i.e., inconsistently, and contradicting myself in the reasoning upon which I act. Put like this, however, the demands of the moral law do not seem so very overpowering. While it is no doubt important to be rational and avoid inconsistency, contradiction, or incoherence in what we say and do, if the cost of so doing is certain to be personal misery (as we are imagining), there is surely at the very least equal reason to abandon pure practical rationality.

Kant would probably have denied that there is a problem here. On his view, once our duty has been discerned, only those who are morally insensible will fail to 'reverence the law'. There is no further reason to be found or given for doing what duty requires of us. But what of the possible conflict between duty and happiness? If duty can require us to sacrifice our happiness, don't we need some basis to choose between the two? To appreciate Kant's answer here, we need to see his philosophy in the context of its background belief that our duty is part of a natural harmony of purposes by which God ensures that no conflict between duty and happiness comes about. Indeed, Kant thought that the best argument for God's existence we can have arises from the fact that practical reason must presuppose a God who can and will ensure that duty and happiness do not in the end conflict, whatever immediate appearances suggest.

Something of this idea will be explored further in Chapter Six. Most philosophers, however, have not followed Kant along this theological path. They have tried to defend a non-religious conception of morality and for them the problem remains— why should I follow the dictates of duty at the expense of happiness? This is in fact the reverse of the problem that we encountered in the examination of egoism, hedonism, and eudaimonism. There we saw that a reason is needed to persuade us to abandon all our customary scruples or sense of right and wrong in favour of what we want or what would give us pleasure. Here, on the other hand, we are in search of a reason to abandon all our natural concern with happiness in obedience to the demands of something called 'the moral law'. And the Kantian non-theological answer to this question—obedience to the moral law for its own sake is a requirement of pure practical reason—does not seem sufficiently weighty to override the natural considerations in favour of happiness.

It may well be argued, of course, that all the fault arises from focussing upon worthiness to be happy rather than upon happiness itself. In fact, some philosophers have thought that morality is centrally concerned with happiness; that the morally good person is not the person like Kant who strives to obey an abstract, rational law indifferent to the welfare of human beings as we find them, but rather the person who seeks in all they do to realize 'the greatest happiness of the greatest number of people'. This last expression is, in fact, the slogan of an alternative but no less influential school of moral philosophy—utilitarianism—and this is the subject of our next chapter.

SUGGESTED FURTHER READING

Original Sources
David Hume, *A Treatise of Human Nature*, esp. book 2, part 3, sect. 3, and book 3, part 1
Immanuel Kant, *Foundations of the Metaphysics of Morals*

Commentary
Jonathan Harrison, *Hume's Moral Epistemology*
H J Paton, *The Categorical Imperative*

Contemporary Discussion
Alasdair MacIntyre, *After Virtue*, chaps. 4–6
Richard Taylor, *Good and Evil*, chap. 8
Bernard Williams, *Ethics and the Limits of Philosophy*
Peter Winch, *Ethics and Action*, chaps. 7–8

CHAPTER FIVE

THE MORAL LIFE II: UTILITARIANISM

The last chapter concluded that Kant's conception of the best human life as one lived in accordance with moral duty pursued for its own sake encounters serious difficulties. Three of these difficulties are specially important. First, it seems impossible to disregard the successfulness of our actions in deciding how well or badly we are spending our lives. Second, Kant's categorical imperative, by means of which we are supposed to determine what our duty actually is, is purely formal, and vastly different ways of life can be made to be in accordance with it, including some that most people would regard as wicked. Third, the divorce between a morally virtuous life and a personally happy and fulfilling life, and the emphasis upon *deserving* to be happy rather than actually *being* happy, leaves us with a problem about motivation. Why should anyone aspire to live morally, if doing so has no necessary connection with living happily?

If these are indeed major problems with the 'duty for duty's sake' conception of a good life, we might suppose that a more successful conception is to be obtained by giving pride of place to happiness and our success in bringing it about. This is just what utilitarianism, the major rival to Kantian moral theory, does. In order to understand the importance of utilitarianism properly, something needs to be said about its origins. We can then consider its merits as a way of thinking about good and bad, right and wrong.

UTILITY AND THE GREATEST HAPPINESS PRINCIPLE

The term 'utilitarianism' first came to prominence in the early nineteenth century, but not as the name of a philosophical doctrine. It was rather the label commonly attached to a group of radical English social reformers at whose instigation many important social measures were passed. The term derives from the word 'utility', meaning 'usefulness', and the social reformers were labelled in this way because they made the practicality and usefulness of social institutions the touchstone of their policies. But their idea of what was useful and practical did not always coincide with the interests of those who had to live with the institutions they reformed. It was the utilitarians who were behind the dreaded institution of the workhouse, which replaced the old Elizabethan Poor Law, and into which the poor and unemployed were often obliged to go. Under this new system, the poor were not left in their own localities and given financial assistance by town officials, as they had been since the time of Queen Elizabeth I, but were compelled to move into large institutions where food, lodging, and employment were provided under one roof. Hence the name 'workhouse'. Throughout the early and middle decades of the nineteenth century, workhouses were constructed in many parts of England and Wales. These may have served social 'utility' better than the ramshackle workings of the Poor Law, for they took vagabonds off the street and enabled financial limits to be put on the total cost of welfare. But the poor greatly feared the prospect of the workhouse, and the misery and degradation of those who lived in many of them, most famously portrayed by Charles Dickens in *Oliver Twist*, has become an indelible part of our image of Victorian England. It is this rather harsh conception of utility that lies behind the modern meaning of 'utilitarian', nowadays defined as "concerned with usefulness alone, without regard to beauty or pleasantness" (*Chambers Dictionary*).

This definition and the popular picture of the Victorian

workhouse, however, are quite inappropriate when we consider the philosophical doctrine called utilitarianism, because its chief concern is with general happiness rather than social convenience. The philosophical doctrine is in fact somewhat misnamed, since, far from ignoring pleasure and happiness, its most fundamental doctrine is that 'that action is best, which procures the greatest happiness'. This famous expression, generally known as 'the Greatest Happiness Principle' predates the label 'utilitarianism' by several decades. It is to be found first in the writings of Francis Hutcheson (1694–1747), an Irish Presbyterian minister who became Professor of Moral Philosophy at the University of Glasgow in Scotland (where he had the distinction of being the first professor in Scotland to lecture to his students in English rather than Latin). Hutcheson wrote a celebrated treatise entitled *Inquiry into the Original of Our Ideas of Beauty and Virtue*, in which the formulation of the Greatest Happiness Principle just quoted is to be found. But Hutcheson's main concern in his writings was elsewhere and he did not develop the Greatest Happiness Principle into a fully elaborated philosophical doctrine. In fact, though he provides the first formulation of its fundamental principle, the founder of utilitarianism is usually thought to be the English jurist Jeremy Bentham.

JEREMY BENTHAM

Jeremy Bentham was a very remarkable man. He went up to the University of Oxford at the age of twelve and graduated at the age of fifteen. He then studied law and was called to the bar at the age of nineteen. He never actually practised law, however, since he very soon became involved with the reform of the English legal system, which he found to be cumbersome and obscure in its theory and procedures as well as inhuman and unjust in its effects. His whole life, in fact, was devoted to campaigning for a more intelligible, just, and humane legal system. In the course of this life, he wrote many thousands of pages. However, he wrote in a very fragmentary style, often abandoned a book before he had finished it, and did not bother about its publication even if he did finish it. Several of the few books that did appear in his lifetime were first published in France by an enthusiastic French follower. The result is that Bentham left relatively little in the way of sustained theoretical writings. Nevertheless, he was the chief inspiration of the radical politicians of his day. He also founded an influential journal, the *Westminster Review*, and established University College London, where his mummified body, with a waxen head, is still on public view.

Bentham was more of a legal and constitutional theorist than a philosopher. Not only did he study constitutions, he also drew them up, and his services were occasionally sought by newly founded republics who wanted written constitutions. Bentham made the basis of his recommendations 'utility'. By this he meant not '*usefulness* without regard to pleasantness' but rather

that property in any object, whereby it tends to produce benefit, advantage, pleasure, good or happiness, (all this in the present case comes to the same thing) or (what comes again to the same thing) to prevent the happening of mischief, pain, evil, or unhappiness. (*Introduction to the Principles of Morals and Legislation*, p. 126)

Such was Bentham's influence on subsequent philosophical theory that while in common speech 'utilitarian' still means what *Chambers Dictionary* says it does, a philosophical utilitarian is one who believes in promoting pleasure and happiness. Bentham believed, as he tells us in his *Introduction to the Principles of Morals and Legislation*, that

Nature has placed mankind under the governance of two sovereign masters, *pain* and *pleasure*. It is for them alone to point out what we ought to do, as well as to determine what we shall do. (*Introduction to the Principles of Morals and Legislation*, p. 125)

The way to construct successful social institutions, that is, institutions with which people can live contentedly, is to ensure that they produce as much pleasure and as little pain as possible for those who live under them. Thus expressed, this is, of course, a social or political doctrine rather than an ethical one. However, we can easily extend the same sort of thinking to human actions and hold that the right action for an individual to perform on any occasion is that which will produce the greatest pleasure and the least pain to those affected by it. Bentham himself meant it to encompass both. He goes on to write:

The principle of utility is the foundation of the present work. . . . By the principle of utility is meant that principle which approves or disapproves of every action whatsoever, according to the tendency which it appears to have to augment or diminish the happiness of the party whose interest is in question: . . . I say of every action what-soever; and therefore not only of every action of a private individual, but of every measure of government. (p. 126)

In very much in the same spirit, we can extend the principle of utility to include not just actions, but whole lives. It thus becomes a general view of the morally good life, according to which the best human life will be one spent in maximizing the happiness and minimizing the pain in this world.

One of Bentham's contributions to the theory of utilitarianism was the elaboration of an 'hedonic calculus', a system of distinguishing and measuring different kinds of pleasure and pain so that the relative weights of the consequences of different courses of action could be compared. In this way, he thought, he had provided a rational method of decision making for legislators, courts, and individuals, one which would replace the rationally unfounded prejudices and the utterly whimsical processes from which, in Bentham's view, decisions usually emerge.

From a philosophical point of view, much of Bentham's

thinking is rather primitive. The man who gave the doctrine greater philosophical sophistication was John Stuart Mill, some of whose writings were discussed in Chapter Two. Mill was the son of one of Bentham's close associates, James Mill. Among his many writings is an essay entitled *Utilitarianism*. It is this short work that made 'utilitarianism' the recognized name of a philosophical theory and at the same time provided its most widely discussed version. Here Mill expressly commends a divorce between the common and the philosophical uses of 'utility':

A passing remark is all that needs be given to the ignorant blunder of supposing that those who stand up for utility as the test of right and wrong, use the term in that restricted and merely colloquial sense in which utility is opposed to pleasure. (*Utilitarianism*, p. 256)

This is, he says, a "perverted" use of the term 'utility', and one which has unfairly discredited the 'theory of utility', which he restates as

[t]he creed which accepts as the foundation of morals, Utility, or the Greatest Happiness Principle . . . that actions are right in proportion as they tend to promote happiness, wrong as they tend to produce the reverse of happiness. By happiness is intended pleasure, and the absence of pain; by unhappiness, pain, and the privation of pleasure. (*Utilitarianism*, p. 257)

Mill intended his work to rescue the word 'utility' from corruption, but despite his efforts, the words 'utility' and 'utilitarian' in common speech still mean something opposed to pleasure and only indirectly connected with happiness. But if the terminology of philosophical utilitarianism remains somewhat specialized, the doctrine itself has come to have wide appeal in the modern world. Even a cursory glance at most of the advice columns in contemporary newspapers and magazines, for instance, will reveal that their writers assume the truth of something like the Greatest Happiness Principle. Moreover, they clearly regard such a view as not only correct, but uncontentious and incontestable. Indeed, it is not an exaggeration to say that utilitarianism has come to be the main element in contemporary moral thinking. A great many people seem to suppose there can be no serious objection to the moral ideal of maximizing happiness and minimizing unhappiness both in personal relationships and in the world at large. When actions are prescribed that appear to have no connexion with pleasure and pain (orthodox Jewish dietary restrictions, for instance), or when social rules are upheld that run counter to the Greatest Happiness Principle (Christian restrictions on divorce, for instance), it is those actions or restrictions that are most readily called into question, not the Happiness Principle itself.

And yet, as we shall see, utilitarianism encounters serious philosophical difficulties. In order to appreciate the full force of these difficulties, however, it is first necessary to expound the doctrine more fully by introducing some important distinctions.

EGOISM, ALTRUISM, AND GENERALIZED BENEVOLENCE

Both Bentham and Mill make the principle of utility or Greatest Happiness Principle the centre of their moral thinking. Mill defines happiness in terms of pleasure, and Bentham makes no distinction between the two. This focus upon pleasure may raise a doubt as to whether there is anything new in utilitarianism that has not already been discussed in Chapter Two under the heading of hedonism. Have we not seen already that pleasure and happiness cannot be the foundation of the good life, because people may indulge in loathsome pleasures and have radically different conceptions of happiness? Why do these objections not apply to utilitarianism?

It is true, certainly, that some of the same issues that were discussed in the context of hedonism also arise in the discussion of utilitarianism. If other people have sadistic pleasures, why should I promote them? This and other similar questions will be considered in a later section. But for the moment it is very important to see that, contrary to the impression Bentham's and Mill's emphasis upon pleasure many give, utilitarianism is not an *egoistic* doctrine. It does not give any special importance to the pleasure or happiness of the individual whose actions are to be directed by it. Indeed, Bentham says that in applying the principle, each is to count for one and no one for more than one. What this means is that my pleasures and pains are not to be regarded by me as any more important than yours when it comes to deciding what it is right and wrong for me or for anyone to do. My own pleasures and pains and those of others are to be calculated and compared exactly on a par. Egoism is the doctrine that we have most reason to put our own interests before those of others, and utilitarians insist that everyone's interests should be treated as equal. This ensures that utilitarianism is not an egoistic doctrine.

But neither is utilitarianism altruistic, if by altruism we mean the doctrine that the interests of others should be put before our own interests. Many people have thought altruism to be central to morality. This is no doubt largely because Western morality has been heavily influenced by Christianity, and in most Christian traditions self-denial has been regarded as a virtue. Arguably, Christianity does permit a measure of concern for self alongside concern for others ("Love your neighbour *as yourself*"). In any case, utilitarianism certainly does allow self-concern, since, if what matters is happiness in general, one's own happiness is as important as anyone else's. But it is not any more important. This feature of utilitarianism is usually called its attitude of 'generalized benevolence', a term which is to be contrasted with both altruism and egoism.

As we shall see, there remains a question whether, and on what basis, the requirement to adopt an attitude of generalized benevolence can be shown to be obligatory. Why should I treat my own interests on a par with others, and why must I treat all others on a par? Can I not reasonably favour my children over other people's? But before addressing these questions directly, there are other distinctions to be drawn.

ACT AND RULE UTILITARIANISM

Utilitarianism as Bentham defines it holds that that action is best which leads to the greatest happiness of the greatest number. (Actually, the addition of 'the greatest number' is redundant. If we seek the greatest happiness, numbers will take care of themselves.) It does not take a great deal of imagination, however, to think of special contexts in which this principle would condone some very questionable actions. For instance, children often spontaneously laugh at the peculiar movements of handicapped people, and we teach them not to do so because of the hurt this causes. But from the point of view of the *general* happiness, we would do as well to encourage the laughter. On the assumption that the handicapped are a small minority, the pleasure given to the majority would then outweigh the pain caused and so accord with the Greatest Happiness Principle.

Counterexamples of this sort can be multiplied indefinitely. Imaginary cases show that the strict application of the Greatest Happiness Principle has results that stand in sharp contradiction to commonly accepted opinion. Some of the counterexamples philosophers have devised are rather fanciful, but they make the same point very clearly. Imagine a healthy and solitary tramp who leads a mundane existence and contributes nothing to the common good. If there were in the same vicinity a talented musician needing a heart transplant, a brilliant scientist needing a liver transplant, and a teenager whose life was being made miserable by a defective kidney, on anyone's reckoning the greatest happiness of the greatest number would be served by killing the tramp painlessly and using his organs for the benefit of the other three. But such an action would, of course, be wilful murder of the innocent. It follows that under certain circumstances utilitarianism would not only condone but morally require the wilful murder of innocent people.

In response to counterexamples of this kind, a distinction is usually drawn between 'act' utilitarianism and 'rule' utilitarianism. Whereas the former, i.e., the version Bentham espouses, says that every *action* must accord with the greatest happiness, the latter says that you should act in accordance with those *rules* of conduct that are most conducive to the greatest happiness. Drawing this distinction enables the 'rule utilitarian' to say that, while there may indeed be occasions when an action commonly regarded as abhorrent would contribute more to the general happiness, its abhorrence arises from the fact that it is contrary to a rule that itself is conducive to the greatest happiness. The reason for condemning the wilful murder of the innocent is indeed a utilitarian one, because the absence of such a general prohibition would greatly increase fear, pain, and loss amongst human beings and hence create unhappiness. Moreover, since we cannot be sure of the consequences of each given action, and could not reasonably take time to ponder them in each and every case, we *must* be guided by general rules. And the only acceptable criterion for those rules is a utilitarian one: act in accordance with those rules that, if generally acted upon, will lead to the greatest happiness.

This amendment to the basic 'act utilitarianism' of Bentham was made by Mill. On Mill's view, the biggest stumbling block to utilitarianism was the apparent conflict with justice such as is illustrated by the case of the tramp. But, he claims:

The moral rules which forbid mankind to hurt one another (in which we must never forget to include wrongful interference with each other's freedom) are more vital to human well-being than any maxims, however important, which only point out the best mode of managing some department of human affairs. (*Utilitarianism*, p. 316)

It is the importance of the rules of justice for the happiness of us all, according to Mill, that commonly gives rise to a feeling of outrage when any one of them is broken. But though we have this very strong and special feeling about justice and rights, upon reflection we can see

that justice is a name for certain moral requirements, which, regarded collectively, stand higher in the scale of social utility, and are therefore of more paramount obligation, than any others; though particular cases may occur in which some other social duty is so important, as to overrule any one of the general maxims of justice. (*Utilitarianism*, pp. 320–21)

This version of utilitarianism, the rule utilitarian will say, is not vulnerable to the sort of counterexample so easily brought against the act utilitarian variety because it can explain, always in terms of utility, why some actions are forbidden in general, regardless of the finer measurements of the hedonic calculus. It can also explain the strong feelings people have about justice and injustice, because a concern with what is called justice is vital to everyone's happiness. And it can also explain why, in a few very rare cases, it may be right to overrule the dictates of justice.

In due course we will have to ask whether the distinction between act and rule utilitarianism can be sustained in such a way as to provide a defence against the sort of objection we have just considered. But before we move to a general examination of the doctrine as a whole, there is one more distinction to be introduced and explained.

UTILITARIANISM AND CONSEQUENTIALISM

Rule utilitarianism holds that our actions should be judged according to rules that if followed will have consequences conducive to the greatest happiness, act utilitarianism that actions should be judged directly according to their consequences for happiness. For the moment, let us stick to act utilitarianism. It is important to see that this thesis has two aspects, usually referred to as the hedonic and the consequentialist. The hedonic aspect of it is its concern with happiness, the fact that it makes happiness the ultimate criterion of good and bad, right and wrong. This is indeed an important distinguishing feature, for we have seen that a concern with happiness is not central to every ethical system that has been given serious consideration. Existentialism makes freedom more central, and Kantianism gives pride of place to duty.

But both these other doctrines stand in contrast to utilitarianism in another way; they are neither of them consequentialist. That is to say, for neither of them are the *consequences* of an action the proper basis upon which it is to be judged. Existentialism regards the authenticity or good faith with which an action is performed to be the thing that gives it value, and bad faith to be the thing that detracts from it. Kantianism regards the will behind an action to be what determines its moral value. As a result, in either case we can disregard the consequences when we assess its value.

The difference between consequentialist and nonconsequentialist theories shows up most clearly in the different judgements they sustain in particular cases. Take the well-known example of Don Quixote, Cervantes' famous hero who pursued the loftiest ideals with the greatest enthusiasm but in a hopelessly unrealistic way. In the eyes of a Kantian, provided the ideals and enthusiasm of such a man are of the right kind, the fact that nothing of the ideal is realized, or that havoc may follow in his path, does not matter; he is nonetheless morally worthy. Or consider the actions of someone like the French nineteenth-century painter Gauguin, who deserted his wife and family and sailed to Tahiti to pursue his true calling as an artist. To an existentialist, Gauguin's being true to himself allows us to discount the personal unhappiness he caused others. In neither case is the happiness or unhappiness of others specially important for these theories. This is not just because other things are more important than happiness, but because in passing judgement on Don Quixote or Gauguin, it is not *consequences* that we should be judging, but the *will* with which or the *spirit* in which they did what they did. In taking this view, both theories differ markedly from utilitarianism.

Utilitarian ethics, then, has two important aspects, the hedonic (its concern with pleasure and happiness) and the consequentialist (its focus upon the consequences of action). Moreover, the hedonic and the consequentialist aspects are quite distinct; neither implies the other. We can see this by registering the fact that an evaluative doctrine can be consequentialist without being hedonic and hence without being utilitarian. Consider the case of Gauguin again. Utilitarians are likely to think badly of Gauguin because of the consequences of his action, the pain and anguish he caused (though a utilitarian *could* argue that the pleasure given by his paintings in the longer term has outweighed the pain he caused his family). On another theory concerned with a different *type* of consequence, his action might be thought good precisely because of the consequences. Someone who took the sort of view Oscar Wilde used to espouse and defend on his American lecture tours, a view often called aestheticism, might claim to the contrary that we should think well of Gauguin because his action had good consequences for art and beauty. This sort of aestheticism can be consequentialist in structure, though its overriding concern is with beauty. Its belief is that the best actions are those whose consequences protect and promote beauty to the greatest degree. Since aestheticism so defined cares about beauty more than happiness, it is consequentialist but not utilitarian.

What this shows is that, though utilitarianism is a consequentialist doctrine, utilitarianism is not the same as consequentialism. This opens up the possibility of two different types of criticism. We might criticize utilitarians for their overriding concern with happiness or for their exclusive concern with consequences. If either criticism were found to be substantial, this would signal the refutation of the doctrine as a whole. It is especially important to mark this distinction between the two aspects of utilitarianism. For if to the modern mind the value of happiness cannot be exaggerated, it may yet be the case that the consequences of an action are not all that matter. Whether there are substantial criticisms on either count is a question we shall now have to investigate. Let us begin with consequentialism.

ASCERTAINING CONSEQUENCES

Consider the nature of an action. We are sometimes inclined to think of actions and their consequences as we do of stones thrown into a pond. The stone causes ripples that travel outwards until their force is spent. At this point the stone's effect is ended. But in reality actions are not like that. They do indeed effect changes in the world. By and large that is their point. But the consequences of an action have themselves consequences, and those consequences in their turn have consequences. The consequences of the consequences also have consequences, and so on indefinitely. The position is further complicated when we add negative consequences, that is, when we take into consideration the things that *don't* happen because of what we do as well as the things that do. This addition makes the extension of the consequences of our actions indefinite, and this means that it is difficult to assess them. It may make it impossible, since there is now no clear sense to the idea of *the* consequences of an action at all.

To appreciate these points fully, consider the following example. It used to be said that the First World War was begun by the assassination of the Austrian Archduke Ferdinand in the streets of the Balkan town of Sarajevo. Let us ignore the historical complexities that might cause us to question this claim and suppose it to be true. The assassins were successful because of a mistake on the part of the archduke's driver. It was he who drove up the wrong street and was forced to turn back. As the car halted in order to turn, the assassins got the chance that had evaded them all day. Thus Ferdinand was shot when he would otherwise have been driven safely home, had the driver not made his fateful error.

What are we to say of the driver's action in turning the wrong way? Its immediate consequence was that the archduke was dead. But the consequence of that death was the outbreak of a war in which many millions were slaughtered. That war provoked the Russian Revolution, which eventually brought Stalin to power, and it ended with a peace settlement that treated Germany so harshly that it was a major contributory factor in the rise of Hitler. And with the rise of Hitler came the Holocaust, the Second World War, and the development of nuclear weapons and their use at Hiroshima and Nagasaki. Considered from a utilitarian point of view, that one simple error must have been the worst action in history by a very wide margin.

Of course, there is something both monstrous and absurd about attributing responsibility for this vast chain of consequences to the archduke's driver. To begin with, it must cross our minds to wonder whether most of the same events would not have happened anyway. Another equally natural response is to say in the driver's defence that his was an unintentional mistake and that it was the assassins, after all, who deliberately committed the murder. To respond in this second way is revealing. It has two distinct aspects. The first part of the defence looks beyond the *consequences* to the driver's *intentions*. The fact that this is a very natural response shows how contrary it is to deep-seated ways of thinking to assess an action *solely* in terms of consequences. The second part of the defence suggests that the chain of consequences may not be the same as the chain of responsibility. The assassination of the archduke was certainly a consequence of the driver's mistake, but perhaps it does not follow from this that he is to be held responsible. The driver was responsible for the car's being halted in a side road, but it was the assassins who decided to fire. Why should the driver be saddled with responsibility for their decision?

Both these lines of thought are important, but a third objection to consequentialism observes that if we are to trace its consequences indefinitely in this way, we may as easily go back beyond the driver's action and construe it as a consequence of someone else's action. Why start the chain of consequences with him, rather than the superior officer who assigned him to that duty? And why stop there? Why not see this assignation as the consequence of the actions of the person who appointed the superior officer? And so on indefinitely.

ASSESSMENT AND PRESCRIPTION

To these criticisms, a consequentialist might reply as follows. We must distinguish between the appeal to consequences in *assessing* an action after it has taken place and the anticipation of consequences in recommending or *prescribing* a course of action. If it really is true that most of the worst aspects of twentieth-century European history were consequences of that hapless driver's mistake, then it was indeed an appalling error. But of course consequences on this scale could not be foreseen at the time, and the driver cannot properly be accused of acting *so as to bring about* those consequences. In deciding to turn the car, he made a fateful decision, but at the time he acted rightly if, as far as he could see, such a decision was likely to have good consequences. Concern with consequences *before* the event can obviously only be with *anticipated* consequences, whereas the concern with consequences *after* the event is with *real* consequences. As a result, strange though this may sound, it can be right to perform an action that turns out to have been wrong, because 'wrong' here just means ineffective.

If we observe this distinction between assessment and prescription, a consequentialist might argue, we do not get the absurd or monstrous results that the example of the archduke's driver purported to reveal. So long as we are clear that it is an assessment we are making, we can ask about the actual consequences of the driver's mistake independently of his responsibility for those consequences. The reason for taking his action as the starting point of our assessment, and not looking further back to the things that gave rise to it, is just that we have chosen to ask about the consequences of that action and not an earlier one. We can just as easily ask about the consequences of the assassins' action and find these to be horrific, too. There is no uncertainty here, provided we are clear about which action or event it is whose consequences we want to assess.

When it comes to holding people responsible, on the other hand, the position is quite different. If we enter imaginatively into the driver's situation, we have to decide what, as consequentialists, it would be sensible to prescribe as his best action at the time and in the circumstances prevailing. Pretty plainly, having made his mistake, the recommendation would be that he should turn the car in order to take the archduke back safely. He was not to know that assassins would by chance enter the same street at that moment. Therefore, because the *anticipated* consequences were good, even though the *actual* consequences were not, he chose rightly.

This distinction between deciding how to act and assessing how we have acted is obviously of the greatest importance for consequentialism, because we cannot know the consequences of our actions before we have taken them. As a result, a doctrine restricted to assessment after the event would have no practical application. But if we cannot assess actual consequences before the event, how are we to decide what to do? The answer is that we have to rely upon generalizations about cause and effect and follow general rules. We estimate the likely consequences of a proposed course of action on the basis of past experience, and we summarize our experience in useful general rules of conduct.

OBJECTIONS TO CONSEQUENTIALISM CONSIDERED

Does the distinction between assessment and prescription overcome the objections to consequentialism it was intended to meet? The first objection, that any action has an indefinitely long chain of consequences that it would be impossible to anticipate or assess, raises some very deep and difficult philosophical questions about cause and effect. Fortunately, I do not think we need to get embroiled in these for present purposes. Whatever way one looks at it, we can say with certainty that shooting people hurts and often kills them, and frequently brings misery and grief in its train. We may be unsure just how far to trace the consequences of an action, or, rather, which of the many consequences are relevant to moral assessment. It is plain, however, that we are indeed able to make limited judgements of this sort. Perhaps for practical purposes it is always necessary to draw a somewhat arbitrary line when estimating consequences, but so long as we can make some such estimate, we can raise the question whether it is chiefly or solely the agreed consequences of the action that matter. Consequentialists say it is, and others such as Kant say it is not. The dispute between them can arise whenever relevant consequences are agreed upon. Thus any difficulty about estimating *the* consequences in a more absolute sense cannot settle that dispute in favour of either party. In short, there is certainly a metaphysical difficulty about the idea of 'the' consequences of an action, but it is one which need not trouble ethical consequentialism, since in practice the morally relevant consequences of an action are usually agreed upon.

The second problem is not so easily circumvented, however. This is the objection that it is unreasonable to say that people have acted badly because of consequences that were not merely unforeseen but unforeseeable. We can usefully return here to an example from the last chapter. Imagine someone who raises money and dispatches medical supplies to some disaster-stricken part of the world. The medicines are badly stored and as a result become contaminated. The consequence is that those who are given them fall horribly ill and in the end more people die than if no supplies had been sent in the first place. The Kantian thinks this sort of example shows that con-sequences are irrelevant to the moral merits of the action.

The consequentialist would reply, however, that conse-quences *are* relevant even to examples of this sort. What makes the action praiseworthy is that it was an attempt to prevent pain and promote health and happiness, i.e., an action whose *probable* consequences were good. Certainly, it is not enough for people to mean well; they must actually be motivated by an accurate estimate of likely consequences. What makes such a principle of action praiseworthy, consequentialists think, is the fact that, special cases apart, acting upon *anticipated* good consequences generally leads to *actual* good consequences.

But this reply raises a further difficulty, which philosophers usually refer to as 'the problem of spontaneity'. Is it true that if in general people try to anticipate the consequences of their actions, this itself will tend to lead to good consequences? Take the case of children falling into ponds or rivers. If potential rescuers pause to take stock and estimate the consequences of any attempted rescue, in most cases the children will drown. Similarly, in the case of plane crashes or earthquakes, time taken up in consideration of the consequences will very likely increase the death toll. If more lives are to be saved in circum-stances such as these, what is needed is spontaneity on the part of the rescuers, a willingness *not* to stop and think but to act spontaneously. Of course, spontaneous action does not always lead to the best consequences. I may save someone from death but thereby condemn him or her to a life of constant pain and misery. Or I might unwittingly pull a future Hitler from the flames. And had I stopped to calculate, these results might have been anticipated. This shows that sometimes it would be useful to estimate consequences. The trouble is that we cannot know these occasions in advance and so the general good is better served if we do *not* try to estimate the consequences of our actions.

This is a curious conclusion. Though in retrospect the

moral quality of an action is to be assessed in terms of consequences, at the time of its performance what matters is the unreflective belief that that is the action that ought to be performed. More lives will be saved if people uncritically believe that you ought to try to save life whatever the consequences. In this way, it seems, the consequentialist doctrine (act so as to bring about the best consequences) is worthless as a guide to action. In other words, if what has been said about spontaneity is true, the belief that consequences ultimately matter requires us *not* to be practising consequentialists.

If we extend this line of reasoning from consequentialism in general to utilitarianism in particular, we must conclude that a belief in the Greatest Happiness Principle requires us not to be practising utilitarians at least some of the time. The greatest happiness will not always be served by those who spend time and effort on hedonic calculations but sometimes by those who spontaneously follow their own best instincts.

ACT AND RULE UTILITARIANISM RECONSIDERED

At this point a utilitarian will be tempted to reply that throughout this discussion the crucial distinction between act and rule utilitarianism has been overlooked. While an act utilitarian, it will be recalled, believes that every action should be taken so as to maximize happiness, the rule utilitarian thinks that our actions should be determined by rules which, if generally followed, would lead to the greatest happiness. So a rule utilitarian might say this. It is true that people ought not to pause on each and every occasion to ponder the consequences of their actions. For one thing, we are not always able to estimate the consequences of our actions with any degree of accuracy, and, for another, the general welfare and happiness does often need people to act spontaneously on their own best instincts. But all this shows is that people should follow general rules of conduct, and should often do so in a wholly unreflective and intuitive way. It is, however, *utilitarian* rules that they should follow, rules fashioned in accordance with the welfare and happiness of all.

It should now be apparent that the distinction between act and rule utilitarianism is a very important one because it has been called upon to provide the means of replying to two serious objections. To the objection that utilitarianism too readily justifies the use of unjust means to utilitarian ends (our example was the murder of a tramp to provide others with vital transplant organs), the rule utilitarian replies that the rules and the deep sense of justice that this sort of counterexample appeals to are both to be explained in terms of the Greatest Happiness Principle. Second, to the objection that it would be a bad thing if our every action were guided by the Greatest Happiness Principle, the rule utilitarian replies that our actions should be guided by an adherence to rules that are themselves justified by appeal to the Greatest Happiness Principle.

It is thus very clear that a great deal rests upon the rule version of utilitarianism. And yet some philosophers have argued that the distinction between act and rule utilitarianism cannot ultimately be sustained to the purpose for which it was introduced. The argument goes like this: Take a rule such as 'Never punish the innocent'. To many people, this seems a fundamental principle of justice, but on a utilitarian account the force of this rule, whether or not we call it a rule of justice, arises from its important connexion with social utility. The greatest happiness of the greatest number of people in society at large will best be served if officers of the law consider this rule inviolable. Now consider a very familiar sort of counterexample.

In a frontier town, three children have been abducted, sexually assaulted, tortured, and murdered. There is an enormous public demand that the local sheriff find the murderer. As time goes on and no one is arrested, public fear increases, unrest grows, and confidence in the forces of law and order diminishes. A man is arrested, and such is the circumstantial evidence against him that it is widely believed that the real murderer has been found. It becomes clear to the sheriff that the man he has arrested is innocent and ought to be released, but a lynch mob has gathered and is threatening to tear down the jail house unless the suspect is tried and executed or handed over. There is no immediate possibility of a fair trial, but it looks to the sheriff as though serious public disorder and considerable damage and injury are likely if he tries to resist the demands of the lynch mob. Should he execute or hand over to the mob a man he knows to be innocent?

Most people would recognize this as a real dilemma. Nor should its imaginary nature mislead us. Dilemmas of this sort are common in the modern world. The following sort of case is only too familiar. Terrorists have taken innocent hostages and are about to detonate a bomb that will kill and injure many hundreds of people. The only way to stop them is to destroy their headquarters, killing the hostages at the same time. In contexts of this kind, it is easy to *say*, 'Let justice be done, though the heavens fall' (*fiat justitia, ruat caelum*) until there is a a real prospect of the heavens' falling. What is of interest here, however, is not how dilemmas like these are to be resolved but how they are to be analysed. A non-utilitarian who believes that justice cannot be reduced to or even explained in terms of utility will think that what we have is a straightforward clash between the general welfare and the rights of the innocent, in short between utility and justice. It is this clash that makes these cases dilemmas.

In sharp contrast, an act utilitarian cannot see any element of dilemma at all. If the balance of general good over individual loss has been properly described, then it is as clear as anything could be that we should sacrifice the innocent. From the point of view of act utilitarianism, these cases are in principle no different from any other calculation about good and bad consequences, and if the good outweighs the bad then there is nothing wrong with our action. There is no dilemma to agonize over.

Few people would accept this view of the matter and are

therefore inclined to reject act utilitarianism. It is rejection on these grounds that Mill and subsequent rule utilitarians have hoped to forestall. For the appeal to moral *rules*, it is claimed, can explain both why we think there is a dilemma in this sort of case and how we are to resolve it. The claim is that in killing the innocent in these special circumstances, though we may be acting for the best, we are nonetheless violating a firmly held rule to which deep feelings are attached. And this rule is itself based on considerations of utility. This is Mill's account of the matter. He says of cases involving the rights of innocent parties:

To have a right . . . is . . . to have something which society ought to defend me in the possession of. If the objector goes on to ask, why it ought? I can give him no other reason than general utility. If that expression does not seem to convey a sufficient feeling of the strength of the obligation, nor to account for the peculiar energy of the feeling, it is because there goes to the composition of the sentiment, not a rational only, but also an animal element, the thirst for retaliation; and this thirst derives its intensity, as well as its moral justification, from the extraordinarily important and impressive kind of utility which is concerned. (*Utilitarianism*, pp. 309–10)

Cases like those of the lynch mob and the innocent hostages, then, are explained by Mill as a conflict between rational calculation of utility and a deep 'animal' attachment to a rule which is itself, in general, closely bound up with utility. But this account leaves one important matter unexplained. Why should we have the rule 'Never punish the innocent'? Mill's answer is that in general this rule serves social utility. But plainly it does not always serve it, as the frontier town sheriff's dilemma shows. So from the point of view of social utility the following rule would serve social utility better: 'Never punish the innocent unless serious social strife needs to be averted thereby'. Between *this* rule and the particular case, however, there is no conflict, since this more specific rule allows the handing over of the innocent man to the lynch mob.

If so, there is a very important implication to be drawn. The whole point of the rule version of utilitarianism is that it purports to offer an alternative to the unacceptable act version. But now we have seen that it does not really do so. Faced with cases like those we have been considering, act utilitarians can offer no explanation of why we think there is a dilemma. But neither can rule utilitarians. They may claim that the dilemma arises because there is a conflict between what utility demands in the particular case and what is demanded by the normal social rule governing cases of that sort. We have just seen, however, that any such conflict can readily be eliminated by carefully refining the rule to take account of these special circumstances, in other words by coming up with a different rule. It follows that on the rule utilitarian account of the matter there *is* no real dilemma. Thus rule utilitarianism offers no more of an explanation than act utilitarianism.

SUMMARY: DOES THE END JUSTIFY THE MEANS?

We saw earlier that utilitarianism is a consequentialist doctrine, one according to which it is the consequences of actions that matter from a moral point of view. Though there is more to utilitarianism than this, this consequentialist aspect gives rise to important questions and difficulties. In the last few sections, we have been exploring these difficulties in some detail, but they can be summarized around the age-old question, 'Does the end always justify the means?' Is an action always justified if it has good consequences, regardless of the intention with which it was carried out or the kind of action it is? Consequentialists may differ over what kind of consequences they regard as good, but they must agree in thinking that, since consequences are what matter, the end *does* justify the means. The arguments we have considered suggest that this is wrong.

In the first place, we cannot sensibly speak of *the* consequences of an action. And even if we agree what to regard as the relevant consequences of an action, we cannot explain responsibility simply by following chains of consequences. We also need to consider aims and intentions. Second, sometimes the exclusive pursuit of good consequences seems to require us to undertake courses of action that run counter to our sense of justice. In these cases we need, at the very least, an explanation of the dilemma we feel. A theory such as act utilitarianism, which takes the consequences of each individual action to be what matters, cannot do this. At best it explains why we *think* there is a dilemma when, in reality, there is none. This is just the objection that rule utilitarianism aims to overcome. What the argument of the last section showed is that it does not do so. If we focus solely on the utility of the consequences, we will always have reason to prefer a rule that permits rather than forbids these objectionable actions.

Most people find these objections to consequentialism in general and utilitarianism in particular to be highly persuasive. It should be recognized, however, that they are not conclusive. Like some of the objections to other theories we have encountered, they rely upon a conflict with widely held views. To be consistent, we must reject consequentialism if we are to persist with common views about responsibility, justice, and so on. But we could with equal consistency hold on to consequentialism and reject commonly held views. This does not necessarily mean that we can hold on to utilitarianism, because there is another aspect of it yet to be considered, the hedonic aspect. It is to this we now turn.

THE NATURE OF HAPPINESS

Since almost the beginning of its history, philosophers have wondered whether the idea of happiness upon which utilitarianism depends so heavily can be made sufficiently clear and precise to do the job the doctrine requires of it. Many of these criticisms, it seems to me, can be answered fairly easily, others less easily, and others perhaps not at all. It will be best to consider these in order.

Presented with the Greatest Happiness Principle, people often wonder what exactly happiness is. Neither Bentham nor Mill is very helpful here, because both identify happiness with pleasure and, as we saw in Chapter Two, this is a mistake. But the fact that there is some confusion in these two writers should not lead us to the conclusion that we cannot ourselves be clear about what we mean by happiness. In fact, the application of utilitarianism to everyday life does not need an explicit account of happiness. It is enough if we are able to tell happiness and unhappiness in ourselves and others, and able to distinguish between happy or unhappy resolutions to difficulties and alternative resolutions with different merits or demerits. For instance, we can usually distinguish happy and unhappy marriages. When a marriage is an unhappy one, the question of divorce often arises. In such cases, it is often said happiness is more important than keeping marriage vows. The fact that such a claim can easily be made is evidence that, even in the absence of a general account of what it is, happiness can enter into moral deliberation.

Sometimes it is suggested that there is no one thing which we can label 'happiness'. Different activities and styles of life appeal to different people and what makes one person happy may make another miserable. To try to act for other people's happiness is to court error, and to work for happiness in general may be impossible. That people differ in what makes them happy is obviously true. One woman may be happiest at home surrounded by children. To another, the same style of life is nothing short of captivity. But nothing follows from this about promoting happiness. In the example just given, there is nothing to suggest that a domestically inclined woman cannot recognize this difference. She is not bound to regard the promotion of happiness as the universal prescription of a way of life that suits her. Indeed, she might readily oppose the legal or social imposition of her ideal of wife and mother, precisely on the grounds that it makes too many women unhappy.

Such differences are real but do not impair our ability to

tell happiness from unhappiness and hence our ability to act on the Greatest Happiness Principle. Moreover, it is worth reminding ourselves that though there are these differences, in general there is also a wide measure of similarity in the things that make for human happiness. By and large sickness, injury, bereavement, hostility, and insecurity are obstacles to happiness that anybody will find difficult to overcome. From this, it follows that in practical deliberation there are at least some general guidelines we can follow for the promotion of happiness.

MEASURING HAPPINESS

Neither the absence of a general account of what constitutes happiness, nor the existence of differences in what makes human beings happy, presents a substantial difficulty for utilitarianism. But a critic may point out that utilitarianism requires much more than an ability to tell happiness when we see it. The theory also requires that it be *measurable*. Someone who accepts that we can tell happiness from unhappiness easily enough may well deny that we can quantify it. And yet this is what we must be able to do if we are to apply the Greatest Happiness Principle. If we are to promote the greatest happiness, we must have some way of estimating and adding up the happiness that each individual will get as a result of alternative courses of action if we are to achieve the *greatest* happiness.

The idea of measuring happiness or pleasure (for to him they amounted to the same thing) figures prominently in the thinking of Bentham. As we saw earlier, he tried to think out what later became known as an 'hedonic calculus', a list of dimensions along which pleasure should be measured. In the fifth chapter of his *Principles*, he distinguishes between different sources of pleasure according to their intensity, duration, and so on, and suggests how these are to be ranked in importance. We will not inquire here into the details of his scheme. One thing that is important to observe about it is that, though the name it subsequently was given may be thought to imply the contrary, there are no numerical calculations in it. Indeed, Bentham does not use numbers at all, but only makes comparative judgements.

It is true that later utilitarians did use numbers, especially those who introduced utilitarian concerns into economics. Indeed, the principal achievement of one of the most prominent, an English economist called Jevons, just was to introduce mathematical techniques to economic theory, and one of the effects of this was the practice of representing interpersonal comparisons by graphs. The term used by the economists was not pleasure or happiness, but 'utility', and it is this term that has stuck. Economists still talk of 'marginal utility curves'. Whether what they say in this connexion has much to do with the Greatest Happiness Principle is debatable, but there is no doubt that they require measurable quantities in order to theorize in the way they do. And to many who are unimpressed by the earlier objections, there really is something absurd in supposing that human happiness can be added up and represented on a graph!

But it is easy to mistake the true role of numbers here. No serious philosopher or economist has supposed that either pleasure or happiness can be measured in the way that sugar, or rainfall, or earth tremors can. Nor does anybody think we might devise an instrument of measurement. What Bentham thought was that different pleasures could be *compared* in such a way as to bring out their relative importance, and there is nothing absurd about this idea. Such comparisons are being made every day, for instance by children who have limited pocket money to spend and have to decide what purchase would give them more satisfaction, or tourists whose holiday is coming to an end and have to decide which trips would be more pleasurable. In general, human beings have to make comparisons of pleasure in a host of different contexts, not just for themselves but for others. In choosing a surprise for your birthday, I will have to decide which out of the alternatives would give you more pleasure. Even if, unlike Bentham, we distinguish between pleasure and happiness, we still find that making comparisons of degrees of happiness is something we do all the time. Parents may have to decide at which school a child would be happier. Children may have to decide whether it would make for the greater happiness of all concerned for aging parents to enter a retirement home.

Now if such comparisons can be, and regularly are made, there is no reason why they should not be represented by the use of numbers. Suppose I have three courses of action open to me and try to estimate in each case what the impact on everyone's happiness would be. I decide that course A would lead to more unhappiness than course B and that course B would lead to more unhappiness than course C. I have thus ranked the courses. But I might also think that course A would make people very much more unhappy than course C, whereas course B would only make them a little more unhappy. I may now represent this judgement in numerical terms, say by giving A a value of -10, B a value of $+7$, and C a value of $+10$.

To represent the matter in this way may help to make the comparative judgements clearer to myself and others. It might still be doubted of course whether, having employed numerical values, I am thereby enabled to employ the normal range of mathematical techniques, adding, subtracting, multiplying, dividing, and so on. But the important point to stress is that comparative judgements can be made, and can be represented in numbers. This is all that need be meant by the phrase 'measuring happiness', and, if so, another standard objection to utilitarianism falls.

DISTRIBUTING HAPPINESS

We come now to three objections to utilitarianism that are just as familiar but harder to answer than the two considered so far. The first of these has to do with distribution. The Greatest Happiness Principle tells us that every action we perform should promote the greatest happiness of the people affected by it. For the moment, let us accept this recommendation. In deciding what to do with respect to any action, however, there is still a matter to be resolved. How is the happiness that I produce to be distributed? The importance of this question can best be illustrated with an example.

In the past few decades, many governments, especially those in poorer countries, have taken an active hand in what is called 'population control'. In the belief that in a large and expanding population everyone inevitably ends up with a smaller share of the national product, peasants have frequently been encouraged, and sometimes forced, to have smaller families than they would naturally choose. In general, the rationale for this sort of policy has been the greatest happiness principle—the individual's desire to have a large family will contribute to greater economic misery all round. So individual choice must be restricted for the greater happiness of all.

The empirical belief at the heart of this policy—that more people inevitably means poorer people—has come under scrutiny recently. There is, in fact, serious reason to doubt it. (After all, people, even children, are not only consumers but also producers of economic resources.) But suppose it is true. What concerns us here is whether the truth of this belief combined with the Greatest Happiness Principle implies the policy of population control. And, despite appearances and commonly accepted opinion, it does not take a great deal of reflection to see that it does not. Because the Greatest Happiness Principle says nothing about how happiness should be distributed but is only concerned with total happiness, a situation in which many millions live just above subsistence level is as desirable as one in which a much smaller number of people live in relative luxury.

The use of numbers helps us to represent this very clearly. Imagine a population of 100 million people, all of whom have an average income of $1,000 a year. (Let us assume, for the sake of the example, that income is a measure of happiness or welfare.) The total welfare for a year may thus be calculated as 100 billion dollars. Take now a far smaller population, say one million. Each has an income of $100,000 a year. The sum total in a year is also 100 billion dollars. If we were to have a choice between creating either population, the Greatest Happiness Principle would give us no reason to prefer the second to the first. What is worse, if we imagine that in the second population each person's income falls to $80,000, the greatest happiness principle now gives us reason to prefer the large population of low income earners.

It may be replied to this objection that the argument works only if we suppose that what the Greatest Happiness Principle is concerned with is *total* happiness. But nothing in the principle itself requires this, and we are just as free to interpret it in terms of *average* happiness. If we do, this odd conclusion about different populations does not follow. We have reason to prefer a society in which the average rather than the total happiness is higher, as it is in the second population described above.

This shift from total to average happiness does overcome the first version of the objection about distributing happiness. But it does not overcome all objections of this sort. The average happiness in a population is calculated without reference to distribution within the population, and this means that the Greatest Happiness Principle is silent on what appears to be a matter of great importance. Let us assume once more that income is a genuine reflection of welfare. The average income within one society might be $80,000, but the society might be one in which many people's income falls below $1,000. In another society, the average income might also be $80,000, and no one's income falls below $40,000. The first is a society in which there is great wealth but also great poverty. The second is one in which there is no poverty, though less great wealth. Many people would think that faced with a choice we have reason to prefer the second of these societies. This is a matter for argument, perhaps. The point to be made here is that in that argument utilitarianism is silent. Since matters of distribution seem important, its silence on this score may be counted a serious deficiency.

The examples we have been considering have to do with societies and populations at large, but it is not hard to see that the same problem arises when utilitarianism is invoked in a more personal context. We can easily imagine a family in which the happiness of a favoured child is given precedence over that of every other child and contrast it with a family in which every child is treated more or less equally. The result might be, however, that total and average happiness are the same in both families. If so, most people would think that there is reason to prefer the second, and yet utilitarianism has nothing to say on this score. The fact that common sense suggests that in instances of this sort there *is* more to be said, combined with the fact that utilitarianism has no more to say, seems to imply that its exclusive focus on happiness is a mistake. Neither total nor average happiness gives the full story. Fairness in distribution must also be taken into account. This conclusion brings us to the second objection—that the general happiness is not the only or even the principal value with which we should be concerned.

MILL'S 'PROOF' AND PREFERENCE UTILITARIANISM

Why should we suppose, as utilitarianism does, that happiness is the ultimate value? This is a question that John Stuart Mill expressly addresses in the fourth chapter of *Utilitarianism*, where he attempts to provide what he calls a proof of the principle of utility. His opening argument for this 'proof' is very well known.

The utilitarian doctrine is, that happiness is desirable, and the only thing desirable, as an end; all other things being only desirable as means to that end. What ought to be required of this doctrine—what conditions is it requisite that the doctrine should fulfil—to make good its claim to be believed? The only proof capable of being given that an object is visible, is that people actually see it. The only proof that a sound is audible, is that people hear it: and so of other sources of experience. In like manner, I apprehend, the sole evidence it is possible to produce that anything is desirable, is that people do actually desire it. If the end which the utilitarian doctrine proposes to itself were not, in theory and in practice, acknowledged to be an end, nothing could ever convince any person that it was so. No reason can be given why the general happiness is desirable, except that each person, so far as he believes it to be attainable, desires his own happiness. This, however, being a fact, we have not only all the proof which the case admits of, but all which it is possible to require, that happiness is a good: that each person's happiness is a good to that person, and the general happiness, therefore, a good to the aggregate of all persons. (*Utilitarianism*, pp. 288–89)

This argument of Mill's has been much discussed. Some philosophers have thought it relies on an ambiguity in the word 'desirable'. Whereas 'visible' only means 'able to be seen', 'desirable' can mean both 'able to be desired' and 'worthy to be desired'. Once we have been alerted to this ambiguity, we can see that the fact that something is desired is evidence that it is *able* to be desired, but not evidence that it is *worth* desiring.

Other philosophers have argued that, though this is a possible ambiguity, it plays no part in Mill's argument. They construe him as saying that the only evidence that something is worth desiring is that people find it worth desiring, and that there is abundant evidence of this sort for the claim that happiness is desirable. The fact that the interpretation of Mill's argument is uncertain makes any argument for or against utilitarianism that rests solely upon its being read one way less than satisfactory. We will do better, therefore, to consider related implications of the proof, implications that Mill himself considers, and see whether or not these can lead to a more definite conclusion. One of these arises from the observation that, even if we accept Mill's argument as a proof of the value of happiness, nothing in it shows that happiness is the *only* value. This defect is important, however, because there are plainly many things besides happiness that people value as ends, i.e., *for their own sake* and not merely as a means to something else.

Mill's reply concedes that this is so, but he claims that anything we value for its own sake and not as a means we value *as a constituent part* of happiness. Having taken up music, for instance, because of the pleasure we derive from it, we come to value it for its own sake. Music becomes part of what happiness is for us. This reply, however, is fraught with difficulties. Mill himself provides an example that brings these difficulties to the fore. Money is valuable because it is a means to happiness. But sometimes people come to love money for its own sake. Having formerly sought money merely as a means to happiness, being rich comes to be part of what happiness means to them. Or so Mill claims. But if we think a little further on the matter, this analysis becomes very unclear. The idea seems to be that, when money is valued as a means, it is valued because of the things it can buy, whereas when it is a constituent of happiness it is valued in itself. Suppose I spend money on an expensive and fashionable car. The possession of the car makes me happy. Or suppose, being a miser, I keep the money. In this case possession of the money itself makes me happy. In both cases, the possession of something makes me happy. It seems a matter of indifference whether we say in the first case that the possession of the car was a *means to* or a *part of* my happiness. Similarly, it seems a matter of indifference whether we say, in the second case, that the possession of the money is a means to or a part of my happiness. Either way, neither the car nor the money is valued in itself, but only because it makes me happy.

From this it seems to follow that Mill's distinction is no distinction at all. He has not actually managed to accommodate into his scheme of thinking values other than happiness that are valued in themselves. If we persist in the view that there are such values, then the supremacy of happiness has not been shown. But even if Mill's distinction between 'means to' and 'part of' were a good one, there is a further difficulty. It appears that other things that are valued in themselves can *conflict* with happiness, and there seems no reason to suppose that we must prefer the latter.

A familiar example is that of the deathbed promise. Suppose I promise a dying man that, once he is dead, I will set the record straight, so to speak, by telling his wife and family of his numerous but secret infidelities with the wives of friends and colleagues. Once he is dead, he cannot be pained or distressed by my failure to keep my word. (Let us ignore complications about life after death.) On the other hand, his wife and family and former lovers will all face distress and embarrassment. The happiness principle demands that I break my promise to the dying man. Yet I may feel that fidelity to that promise and to truthfulness in general is more important than happiness. What has Mill to say on the other side?

What he does say (though not in connexion with this specific example) is that I desire to tell the truth because I would be happiest doing so. But this need not be the case. Perhaps the act of revealing the dead man's sins is deeply distressing to me, not least because of my former attachment to him. Mill seems to say at this point in the argument that if I desire to tell the truth, it *must* be the happiest course for me, because "to think of an object as desirable (unless for the sake of its consequences), and to think of it as pleasant, are one and the same thing" (*Utilitarianism*, p. 293). This is, of course, a dogmatic assertion on his part. The issues it raises, and the reasons for rejecting it, however, have already been discussed in Chapters One and Two. We need not labour them here, therefore. The conclusion to be drawn is that Mill has not succeeded with his 'proof' of the supremacy of the value of happiness.

The difficulty of proving the supreme value of happiness has been recognized by some philosophers who have nevertheless wanted to hold on to the general structure of utilitarianism. Acknowledging that Mill's equation of desire and pleasure is without foundation, they have suggested that we might express the whole doctrine not in terms of happiness but in terms of desire satisfaction or preferences—the right action is that which leads to the satisfaction of the greatest number of desires. This version of utilitarianism, generally known as preference utilitarianism, has been much discussed and raises many interesting issues. But here there is room to mention only one. If the shift from happiness to desire satisfaction solves any problems, it also creates them. It seems right to say that happiness is a value, and hence the creation of happiness a good thing. The question is whether it is the only, or the supreme, value. But it is not obvious that desire satisfaction in itself is a value at all, just because some desires are bad. If a girl desires to sleep and a man, contrary to his own best instincts and hence to his happiness, has a strong desire to rape someone, I will maximize the satisfaction of desires by bringing the girl to him drugged sufficiently soundly to make her unaware that she has been raped. To act in this way seems unquestionably wrong, and it adds nothing in its favour to observe that at least it maximized the satisfaction of desire.

Like the issues raised by Mill's proof, many of the issues raised by the move to preference utilitarianism have been discussed already in Chapters One and Two. For this reason, they need not be discussed further here. But in any case, even if Mill had succeeded in proving the supremacy of happiness, the examination of utilitarianism would not end there, because there is a third and final objection to be considered.

MOTIVATION AND THE LIMITLESS MORAL CODE

We have seen that both the consequentialist and the hedonic aspects of utilitarianism raise difficulties. Although it has taken some time to explore these properly, both sets of difficulties can be summarized in a similar way. The attempt to focus exclusively on consequences and on happiness fails because other things besides consequences matter and happiness is not the only value. But suppose for the sake of argument it had been shown to everyone's satisfaction that, from the moral point of view, the right action is that which leads to the greatest happiness. We could still ask why we should go in for morality at all.

To some people, this seems a peculiar question. Considered in relation to utilitarianism, it can quickly be made a genuine one. This is because it is not hard to show that the moral life conceived of along utilitarian lines makes demands upon us which we have every reason to resist. These demands arise from its boundlessness. This boundlessness has two aspects. First, within utilitarianism moral questions and moral demands are constant. Second, if happiness is what matters, it cannot matter whose happiness it is. Let us consider these points in turn.

Most people think of moral questions as periodic. That is, we go about our daily lives, within a framework of law and decency, no doubt, but by and large free of moral questions. These do arise, and sometimes arise very acutely. Moral questions are special questions and when they do arise often require a certain amount of agonizing. But they are not forever arising. Such a view of the place and nature of morality may or may not be correct. It is, however, incompatible with a utilitarian view of morality. Since at every moment of my waking life I *could* be engaged in action conducive to the greatest happiness, I am constantly faced by moral questions. For every action I perform, at home, at work, at play, I can and must ask myself— am I doing right? This seems a very demanding life to lead.

A utilitarian might say that the common view of morality is wrong, that moral questions *are* constantly arising. This may be correct, but it is not to the point. If moral demands are constant, this is a reason for asking very seriously, 'Why should I be moral?'

The other aspect of the unlimited character of utilitarianism is, if anything, even more disturbing. It is illustrated by an example first discussed by the English social thinker William Godwin. Godwin was a convinced utilitarian and he saw that the commitment to the greatest happiness could give rise to painful choices. He imagines a case in which the house of the French Archbishop Fenelon, reputed to be a great benefactor of mankind, goes on fire, and the choice is between rescuing Fenelon or rescuing his maid. Godwin thought that the answer was clear; the right thing to do was rescue Fenelon. But a critic reading this raised a question about what Godwin's attitude would be if the maid in question were his grandmother. Godwin replied that in this case, too, the right thing to do would be to rescue Fenelon.

Some people were appalled at this reply, and philosophers have frequently discussed it and cases like it. But the importance of the example is not just as another counterexample to the application of utilitarianism, similar to many of those already encountered. The point rather is that a view of morality like utilitarianism can give rise to occasions when we are called upon, not merely to sacrifice our nearest and dearest, but to treat them exactly on a par with everyone, and anyone, else. Since our friends and relatives matter much more to us than strangers, even those we know to be benefactors, why should we do this?

One familiar answer is that it is morally right. Assuming, contrary to all the objections rehearsed so far, that the utilitarians are correct in their account of morality, this is certainly true. But it is not an answer. Why should we do what is morally right if it requires us to treat those who are special to us as though they were not? It has sometimes been said at this point that the moral law is overriding, something that must take precedence over every other consideration. But this is just another way of asserting that we must do what morality requires. The question is 'Is morality overriding, and if so why?'

Someone who raises this question will not and cannot be satisfied with an answer that appeals to the content of morality itself. This means that no further refinement of utilitarianism (or any other moral doctrine) will answer this question once it has arisen. It follows that, even if all the difficulties and objections we have been considering could be overcome, there would *still* be a question about the ground in which the demands and requirements of utilitarianism are rooted. And this applies to morality as such.

In fact, our examination of utilitarianism has led to the same conclusion as the examination of Kantianism. Even though utilitarianism gives happiness prime importance, we are left looking for a motivating reason to adopt it. The problem lies with morality itself. However we conceive it, whether along utilitarian or some other lines, we can always ask what the basis of morality itself is. One very familiar answer is that morality must be rooted in religion. This is the topic of the final chapter.

SUGGESTED FURTHER READING

Original Sources
Jeremy Bentham, *Introduction to the Principles of Morals and Legislation*
John Stuart Mill, *Utilitarianism*

Commentary
Anthony Quinton, *Utilitarian Ethics*

Contemporary Discussion
J J C Smart and Bernard Williams, *Utilitarianism for and against*
David Lyons, *Forms and Limits of Utilitarianism*

CHAPTER SIX

RELIGION AND THE MEANING OF LIFE

In this final chapter, we arrive at those topics that many people expect philosophy, and moral philosophy in particular, to be specially concerned with, namely God, good and evil, and the meaning of life. We have rightly been led to these topics by an exploration of questions about the good life, but it should be made clear to the reader at the start that it will not be possible to do more than scratch the surface of the many fascinating but complex issues that a philosophical appeal to religion raises. Up to this point, the discussion has taken the form of a fairly rigorous examination of detailed arguments. Here the subject matter is so vast that this will have to give way to the more speculative pursuit of a line of thought. Before addressing the relevant issues directly, however, a general summary of the argument that has brought us to this point may be useful.

THE ARGUMENT SO FAR

We began this book with the question 'What is the best sort of life a human being can live?' The first answer we considered was that given by the egoist: The best life is one in which you get what you want. There are a variety of objections to this answer, but the most important is this. Egoism supposes that our wants and desires are in some sense 'there' waiting to be satisfied, whereas in reality we are often uncertain about what to want. We can quite intelligibly ask not merely about what we *do* want, but about what we *ought* to want out of life. This question, however, egoism cannot answer. It follows that egoism is inadequate as a guide to good living. Though it tells us what to do, given pre-existent desires, it cannot help us critically form those desires.

The second candidate considered was hedonism, the view that the good life is the life of pleasure. Hedonism goes one stage further than egoism since it recommends not merely the pursuit of desires in general, but a certain specific desire—the desire for pleasure. Consequently, hedonism cannot be charged with the sort of emptiness that egoism can. Moreover, it appears to enjoy a head start in arguments about good and bad, because pleasure seems a naturally appealing value upon which to build a philosophy of the good life. But hedonism is not without its own difficulties. We saw in Chapter Two that we can interpret the life of pleasure along the lines of the Cyrenaics, a 'wine, women, and song' sort of life. The trouble is that given the contingent facts of human biology and psychology, sensuous pleasures of an obvious sort bring sensuous pains of an equally obvious sort. In practice, it is impossible to court 'vulgar' pleasures exclusively, since they nearly all carry pains in their wake. This might lead us, as it did the Epicureans, to think of the life of pleasure along more refined lines, and to recommend, for instance, a life in which sampling fine wines is preferred to getting roaring drunk. But if we do make this alteration in our idea of pleasure, we lose the natural appeal that is hedonism's strength, because the Epicurean life, far from being one of self-indulgence, is actually one of considerable self-restraint.

In any case, against either version of hedonism the point can always be made that there is more to life than pleasure. Even more importantly, as Aristotle saw, there is more to *happiness* than pleasure, and it was this observation that led us on to consider the claims of *eudaimonia* or well-being as the supreme value. Aristotle, it will be recalled, defines the well-being of a thing in terms of its natural function or end, and this raises a question for his philosophy of value: can human beings be said to have a function by nature? One interesting response to this question makes appeal to ethology, the relatively recent science that studies animal behaviour in natural habitats. However, the attempt to wed Aristotelian philosophy and modern ethology is not wholly successful, since it leaves unresolved too many disputes between conflicting styles and modes of life.

Though it is both interesting and attractive, the heart of eudaimonism is the attempt to settle questions of behaviour by reference to our nature as human beings, and what its examination revealed was that eudaimonism settles too few of the issues that moral philosophy raises. But even if it settled a great many, it would nevertheless have a very great failing, at least in the eyes of existentialists. On the existentialists' view, what is distinctive about human beings is their freedom from natural determination, their ability to rise above natural constraints, and their responsibility for their own fate and conduct. It is this freedom that eudaimonism ignores and existentialism brings to the fore. In the examination of existentialism, however, problems of a different sort emerged. The 'authentic' life, it seems, is a conception indifferent to content; it is as good to choose the life of an authentic villain as that of an authentic hero, if all that matters is freedom and authenticity.

Kant tries to show that freedom is not all that matters, that rationality matters just as much. He argues that freedom and reason can be reconciled in a duty-centred conception of the moral life. Much that Kant has to say is subtle, but crucially he seems to leave out of the picture the consequences for human happiness. In doing so, he removes any basis which might motivate us to choose the moral life which he so strongly recommends. This is why he speaks of an irreducible 'reverence for the law' as the source of moral motivation, a conception that, as he himself observes, merely states and does not explain our interest in morality.

The failure of Kantian moral theory to provide an account of moral motivation led us to consider a familiar alternative, utilitarianism, a doctrine which gives pride of place to human happiness and might for this reason be expected to overcome the problems Kant's moral philosophy encounters. But in fact the same problem emerges from a critical examination of utilitarianism. Here, too, we are left with this question: What reason have I to promote the general happiness at the expense of my own personal happiness or the happiness of those nearest and dearest to me? Utilitarianism cannot answer this question and as a result cannot, so to speak, assert its authority over us.

It may seem, in the light of this summary, that the argument so far has been disappointingly negative. Six philosophies of value have been examined and every one of them found to be deficient. The net result appears to be that we are no further on than when we started. But in fact this is not so. From almost every stage of the argument, something valuable has emerged, and in the light of the whole we now have a much clearer conception of what it is we are looking for in the way of a successful philosophy of the good life. We know that we must be able to answer the question 'What ought I to want out of life?' This is what our discussion of egoism showed. The discussion of hedonism, on the other hand, showed that there is more to happiness than pleasure, and the discussion of Aristotle and ethology showed that even happiness is not enough as the sole constituent of a good life. As existentialists insist, we must also recognize the claims of freedom and responsibility.

The further discussion of existentialism, however, showed that our freedom is not only the recognition of responsibility to ourselves, but to others. It is personal freedom and responsibility to others that Kant tries to reconcile in his conception of the moral law. One result of his attempt, however, is his failure to take seriously personal happiness. At best Kant sketches a moral life which we only have reason to follow from the point of view of abstract reason. But why act in accordance with reason as Kant conceives it, if it makes us unhappy? Similarly, at best utilitarianism outlines a life of impartial benevolence directed at the happiness of all mankind. But again, why act impartially, if my own happiness suffers? These are, of course, egoistic questions, but nonetheless real for that.

What we can see as a result of the argument, then, is that some way must be found to accommodate the importance of both freedom and happiness, and a rational basis given to the moral demands of others that can satisfy the legitimate demands of egoism. It is precisely for the accomplishment of this task that many people look to religion.

THE AUTHORITY OF MORALITY

The problem faced by either the Kantian or the utilitarian conception of the moral life may be termed a problem about the authority of morality. The Kantian prescription for a good life is this: 'Always act in accordance with what rational thinking shows to be your duty'. The utilitarian prescription is: 'Always act with a view to impartial benevolence'. When either fundamental principle is questioned, there seems nothing further to say; we can only repeat the prescription. 'Why should I act in accordance with what reason shows to be my duty?' 'You just should'. 'Why should I adopt an impartial attitude and regard my own happiness as no more important than anyone else's?' 'You just should'. What appears to be needed is some prudential or egoistic reason of the form 'It's better for *you* if you do'. But when we supply egoistic reasons, these normally appeal to self-centered reasons and are objectionable in just the way that egoism in general has been found to be. The trouble is that abstractly moral reasons seem to lack personal appeal, and concretely prudential reasons seem to lack the right *sort* of authority.

To many thinkers, the way out of this difficulty lies in recourse to the authoritative will of God. It is not difficult to see in outline how this solution is intended to work. If God is creator and loves his creation, if he is both all powerful and all good, what he commands cannot fail to supply both prudential and moral reasons for action. Obedience to the will of God appeals to our rational self-interest—no one could rationally reject the commandments of such a God, because God will unfailingly prescribe the kind of life most conducive to individual well-being. At the same time, since God is perfect, his commandments must also be compatible both with justice and with the well-being of all creation. It seems then that appeal to the will of God is the way to settle the vexing questions of moral philosophy that have defeated the other lines of thought explored so far. God lays down for us the rules of a good life, and he is uniquely placed to do so since he has created the world in which that life is to be led.

Of course, the matter is not as simple as this. From earliest times, those who have appealed to God as a solution to philosophical problems have been plagued by doubts and difficulties. Three are specially important. First of all, *is* there a God who is the sum of all perfections? Second, granted a positive answer to this first question, can we ever know for certain what God wills for us? Third, if we did know the will of God, would this really provide us with a better grounded guide to life than the non-religious philosophies we have just discussed and found wanting. All three of these questions have a very ancient history and have been discussed ever since human beings began to think about philosophical and theological questions. Let us consider each of the three difficulties in turn. For simplicity's sake, I will set out all three in their strongest and most persuasive form before considering what response it might be possible to make to them.

THE PROBLEM OF EVIL

Does God exist? More pages have been written on this question than any other subject in the history of mankind. Philosophers and theologians have developed several distinct arguments in favour of the hypothesis that God exists. Others have claimed the arguments to be invalid, and still others, such as Kierkegaard, have claimed that all such arguments, positive or negative, are worthless from the point of view of true religion. Some of the greatest thinkers of all time have been convinced religionists—Plato, Aquinas, Descartes, Newton—and some have been total sceptics—Hume, Nietzsche, Marx. Others—Spinoza, Kant, Hegel, and Einstein, for instance—have, as a result of their intellectual reflections, subscribed to versions of religious belief that still others of a more orthodox stripe have condemned. Given this state of affairs, it is almost impossible for a short introductory text such as this to enter seriously into any of the issues which belief in the existence of God raises.

However, this does not oblige us to keep silence altogether. It is worth remembering that in the context of the philosophy of value we are interested only in the existence of a God of a certain sort, namely one who can be considered perfect, the source of goodness itself. We can properly restrict the scope of our interest to the connexion between the existence of God and the attempt to discover what the good life is, and in fact this allows us to set aside almost all the traditional arguments for God's existence. Instead, we can concentrate upon one important argument against the idea of a good God, namely the well-known 'problem of evil'.

The problem of evil is not a problem for all religions. Eastern religions such as Hinduism and Buddhism have no place for the concept of God as the Western religions of Judaism, Christianity, and Islam understand it. Even in these religions, the belief in a God whose nature is perfect and who is the source of all things good cannot be said to be unqualified. The actions of Yahweh as represented in the Old Testament are often more like those of an irritable and whimsical tyrant than of a loving heavenly father. (*"The Lord, whose name is Jealous, is a jealous God"*, Moses is told in the book of Exodus.) In Islam, it is the perpetual and inescapable sovereignty of Allah, rather than inexhaustible love, that is the principal focus of concern. (The opening section of the Qur'an says, "*The Praise is to God, Lord of the worlds, the merciful Lord of mercy, ruler of the judgement day*".) It is chiefly in Christianity that great emphasis is placed upon the love of God for his creation ("*God so loved the world that he gave his one and only Son*".) For this reason, Christian philosophers and theologians have been more concerned with the problem of evil than those of any other religion.

The problem has its practical side, and those who believe in the love of God can hardly fail to experience it from time to time. We have only to look at the suffering and destruction that the world at any place or period of history will be found to contain, to find ourselves asking, 'Where is the love of God here?' The practical problem is to trust in God's goodness in the face of human and animal suffering, suffering that sometimes seems to reach immense proportions, as evidenced by the Holocaust or the ravages of Pol Pot, the Cambodian tyrant responsible for the death of over a million people.

But we can also give the problem a philosophical interpretation, and turn it into an argument that generates the firm conclusion that there is no loving God. The philosophical version of the problem is given one of its best known renderings by Hume, some of whose ideas we have already considered.

[God's] power we allow infinite; whatever he wills is executed: but neither man nor any other animal are happy: therefore he does not will their happiness. His wisdom is infinite: he is never mistaken about chusing the means to any end; but the course of nature tends not to human or animal felicity: therefore it is not established for that purpose . . . Epicurus' old questions are yet unanswered. Is he willing to prevent evil but not able? Then he is impotent. Is he able, but not willing? Then he is malevolent. Is he both able and willing? Whence then, is evil? (*Dialogues*, Sec. 10)

If God is all-loving, he will want to put an end to evil and suffering, and if he is all-powerful nothing can stop him from doing so. From the fact that he always wants to eliminate evil (his omnibenevolence), and the fact that he has the power to do so (his omnipotence), it follows that there ought to be no evil in the world. But there *is* evil in the world, and from the undoubted reality of evil we are forced to conclude either that God does not want to eliminate it, in which case he is not all-loving, or else that he cannot, in which case he is not all-powerful. In theological language, the existence of evil demonstrates that God cannot be both omnipotent and omnibenevolent. John Stuart Mill expresses this conclusion very forcibly.

Not even on the most distorted and contracted theory of good which ever was framed by religious or philosophical fanaticism, can the government of Nature be made to resemble the work of a being at once good and omnipotent. ('Nature', *Three Essays*, Collected Works, p. 389)

It is a small step from this conclusion to the non-existence of God altogether. If there is a God at all, that is, a Being worthy to be worshipped, that Being must be possessed of all perfections, and hence must be both omnipotent and omnibenevolent. This the argument from evil has shown to be impossible. It follows that there is no God.

Some people find this argument wholly persuasive, rooted as it ultimately is in the unquestionable facts of experience. Others have tried to find a flaw in it. Whether there is a satisfactory answer or not is a subject we will leave for the moment while we consider the second of the problems outlined above.

THE PROBLEM OF RELIGIOUS KNOWLEDGE

We are exploring the line of thought in which appeal to religion is held out as a means of establishing good and bad, right and wrong, in a way that secular philosophies of value cannot do. Of course, such an appeal can accomplish this only if it delivers clear and certain answers about the right way to live. But this is precisely what mankind's experience of religion suggests it cannot do. If we look to religion for an answer to the problems of right conduct, we must first settle the question 'Which religion?' Arguably, there is no such thing as 'Religion', only religions, and these give quite different pieces of advice. What is permissible under one religious code is impermissible under another, and what is obligatory under one is a matter of total indifference to another.

For example, suppose we ask whether people should live monogamously or polygamously (a genuine question for people in some parts of Africa today). Leaving Mormonism aside, the Christian religion rules polygamy out, holding up monogamy not only as an ideal, but as the only form *holy* matrimony can take. Islam, on the other hand, makes polygamy not only permissible but desirable. Or take another example. Is it important how we prepare our food? Those religions with dietary laws (Orthodox Judaism, Islam, and, to a lesser extent, Sikhism) hold that it is, though they prescribe quite different rules (indeed, the Sikh dietary laws expressly forbid the consumption of meat slaughtered in the Muslim style). For others, Christianity, for instance, the manner in which food is prepared is a matter of indifference, reflecting Christ's remark that it is not what goes into but comes out of a man that defiles him.

The examples could be multiplied almost indefinitely, and what they appear to show is that the appeal to religion as a guide to conduct is unhelpful, since in practice it is an appeal to a vast range of different, and often contradictory, prescriptions for the good life. If 'How should I live?' is the question that interests us, appeal to religion fails by the curious route of providing an embarrassment of answers.

Of course, it can be suggested that we should try to adjudicate between these different answers, to decide which we should accept and which we should reject. But on what grounds are we to do this? Insofar as each religion claims to be based upon divine revelation, through Moses or Jesus or Mohammed, or the Guru Nanak or Joseph Smith, they are pretty much on an equal footing. On this ground alone there does not seem much to judge between them, since the prescriptions of the Pentateuch, the Gospels, the Qur'an or the Guru Granth Sahib (the Sikh scriptures) seem equally likely or unlikely candidates for the mind of God.

The only plausible way open to us for judging between them appears to lie in putting their claims to some other test whose authority we recognize. For instance, we might 'test' the Jewish dietary laws or the Sikh requirements regarding length of hair and beard against the demands of modern hygiene. We might try to assess the implications for human happiness of the Christian ideal of chastity and fidelity to a single partner in a world where contraception has created sexual freedom. Or we might examine the compatibility of Islamic codes of conduct with the free and equal treatment of women. But in each case we would be testing what purports to be the revealed will of God against some other external standard, thereby going beyond religious revelation and ultimately basing our code upon something else—a belief in hygiene, or sexual freedom, or the equality of women. Religion would not be playing the fundamental role.

Our examination of the problem of religious knowledge has thus brought us in fact to the third of the questions outlined above: 'Does religion provide a better grounded guide to the good life than the secular alternatives we have found wanting?' In the examples just given, we were led to try to resolve differences by appeal to non-religious conceptions of the good. That this inevitably happens if we try to appeal from good to God, so to speak, is the conclusion of the oldest philosophical examination of these matters, Plato's Socratic dialogue *Euthyphro*. The dialogue remains one of the best discussions of the issue and for this reason can still function as a focus of the argument at this point.

PLATO AND THE *EUTHYPHRO* DILEMMA

Euthyphro is a very characteristic Socratic dialogue. It takes its name from its central character, a man supposedly expert in the ways of religion, whom Socrates begins to question. The dialogue is set against a rather intriguing background. Euthyphro, a man of widely acknowledged religious devotion, meets Socrates outside a courthouse, and it emerges from the opening remarks of their conversation that Euthyphro is engaged upon the business of prosecuting his own father for murder. On hearing this, Socrates is somewhat astonished and not unnaturally supposes that the murder victim must be someone to whom Euthyphro is closely attached. But Euthyphro replies as follows:

I am amused, Socrates, at your making a distinction between one who is a member of the family and one who is not; for surely the pollution is the same in either case, if you knowingly associate with the murderer when you ought to clear yourself and him by proceeding against him. The real question is whether the murdered man has been justly slain. If justly, then your duty is to let the matter alone; but if unjustly, then proceed against the murderer, if, that is to say, he lives under the same roof with you and eats at the same table. In fact the man who is dead was a poor dependent of mine who worked for us as a day labourer on our farm at Naxos, and one day in a fit of drunken passion he got into a quarrel with one of our domestic servants and slew him. My father bound him hand and foot and threw him into a ditch, and then sent to Athens to ask an expositor of religious law what he should do with him. Meanwhile he never attended to him and took no care about him, for he regarded him as a murderer; and thought that no great harm would be done even if he did die. Now this was just what happened. For such was the effect of cold and hunger and chains upon him, that before the messenger returned from the expositor, he was dead. And my father and family are angry with me for taking the part of the murderer and prosecuting my father. They say that he did not kill him, and that if he did, the dead man was but a murderer, and I ought not to take any notice, for a son is impious [*i.e., acting contrary to good religion*] who prosecutes a father for murder. Which shows, Socrates, how little they know what the gods think about piety and impiety. (*Euthyphro, Dialogues of Plato, Vol. 1*, pp. 39–40)

By lighting on this last remark, Socrates leads Euthyphro to the claim that, unlike the rest of his family, he is an expert on what the gods do and do not require. With a strong touch of irony, Socrates declares himself anxious to become Euthyphro's disciple that he may himself come to be possessed of such great and valuable knowledge, and, with the questions he now raises, the philosophy proper begins. The dialogue falls into three main parts, but since it is the middle section that is of greatest importance in this context, it will be sufficient to outline the contents of the other two sections only briefly.

In the first part of the dialogue, Socrates argues that it is only what *all* the gods agree on that could possibly be a guide to good conduct. It is hard for people in modern times to take much serious interest in talk of 'the gods', but what this section effectively shows is that talk of 'gods' in the plural is redundant, and that any attempt to give the good life a religious basis must appeal to one God.

In the third section, Plato raises interesting questions about the very possibility of a devout life. If God is perfect and lacks nothing, how can we serve him? There is nothing mere mortals can do that would be of any real value to God. At a later point something of this issue will be considered again. Here we can pass it by, because our concern must be with the second section of the dialogue.

In that section, Socrates presents Euthyphro with a dilemma, that is, a question that seems to have only two possible answers, neither of which is acceptable. The dilemma (expressed in more modern language than Plato employs) is this: Is something good because God approves of it, or does he approve of it because it is good?

An example may make the question plainer. Take the

relief of suffering such as is exhibited in the New Testament story of the Good Samaritan. On his way from Jerusalem to Jericho, a man is set upon by thieves. He is robbed of his goods and left for dead by the roadside. A priest comes along, but passes by on the other side for fear of getting caught up in something unpleasant or inconvenient. Likewise a Levite (a very respectable sort of person) passes by. Then a Samaritan comes along. (It is important to know that the Jews of Jesus' time thought badly of Samaritans.) Unlike the other two, he stops and helps the man, taking him to a wayside inn. He even leaves money with the innkeeper to cover the injured man's expenses.

This story has commended itself to generation after generation as an illuminating example of the love of neighbour Christians are commanded to show. But is the Samaritan's conduct good only because it accords with what God commands? Or is it rather that helping the injured is good in itself and this is why God commands it? Plato, writing long before this story was first told, puts the general point this way: Is something holy because it is beloved of the gods, or is it beloved of the gods precisely because it is holy?

Suppose we answer 'yes' to the first alternative, and agree that there is nothing more to the goodness of an action than its being in accordance with the will of God. Then it seems that if God had required us to do the opposite to what we customarily think is right, it would be equally good; if God had commanded the Samaritan to cross the road from Jerusalem to Jericho and aggravate the victim's wounds, this would have been a good thing to do. But to think this is to think that what we take to be good and bad, right and wrong, is not intrinsically so, but quite contingently so, that it is arbitrarily fixed by God. On this view there is nothing good about happiness or wrong about suffering in themselves; it just so happens that God chose to declare these good and bad respectively, and might as easily have chosen to condemn those who are kind and generous and praise those who are malicious or greedy.

Most people are inclined to reject this horn of the dilemma. They think that God commands us to do what is good because it is good, that God does not act in the manner of a Nero or Caligula, wilfully and whimsically commanding one thing when he might as readily command another. Rather, God sees the truth, commands what is *really* good, and forbids those things that are *really* bad.

But if this is so, then the things that are good and evil really are good and evil, whatever God may think of them. It follows that they are thus independent of his will, and hence neither based upon nor determined by it. By trying to avoid making good and evil subject to a capricious will, we are caught on the other horn of the dilemma. God is not after all the foundation of good, but at best its revealer. Whatever he may will, good is good and bad is bad in reality and independently of his will.

The net result is this: We started out in search of something that would ground the claims of morality in such a way as to answer the prudentially oriented questions of the egoist. It was here that the appeal to the authority of God was supposed to help. But what Plato's dialogue shows is that either good and bad are dependent upon the will of God, in which case they are a wholly arbitrary matter, or else they are not wholly arbitrary, in which case there is no room for any appeal to God.

On three counts, then, any appeal to religion as the basis of a good life seems to be ruled out. The reality of evil in the world throws into doubt the very existence of the right sort of God. Great variety amongst the religions of the world and in the ways of life and kinds of conduct they prescribe creates a major difficulty in deciding what sort of good life the appeal to religion would underwrite. Finally, and perhaps most importantly, Plato's arguments in the *Euthyphro* seem to show that even if the first two difficulties can be overcome, religion cannot logically serve as a ground for morality.

RELIGIOUS EXPERIENCE AND RELIGIOUS PRACTICE

Is there any reply to these difficulties? Many philosophers and theologians have thought so, but once more it will not prove possible in the present context to enter into a detailed consideration of the many replies and counterreplies that have been formulated over the centuries. Here I propose only to gesture towards one very important line of thought.

Let us begin with two striking considerations. The first is this. In the problem of evil, the reality of suffering and misery is presented as a reason for denying the existence of a loving God. In other words, the form of the problem is assumed to be one about hypothesis ('A loving God exists') and evidence ('There is evil in the world'). It is an interesting fact, however, that it is precisely in the experience of suffering and evil—death, disease, bereavement, degradation—that most people turn to hopes of a loving God, turn indeed to religion in general. It seems that the experience of something that is supposed to count as evidence *against* God's existence very often figures as the principal *cause* of that belief. No doubt there are possible psychological explanations of this, but explanations of this sort often assume that people turn to religion in spite of their experience. Why should we not conclude, to the contrary, that the experience has enabled them to see something that might otherwise be missed? If this is true, the traditional construction of the problem of evil must have left something important out of the picture.

The same point may be illustrated in other ways. People are sometimes brought to religious belief by a sense of having been miraculously delivered from some disaster. In every case there is always a simple explanation of how it was that they were not crushed by falling masonry, or how it was that help came upon the scene at just that moment (or whatever). These simple explanations adequately cover the facts of the case, but the people involved very often go further and offer explanations in terms of divine agency. Sceptics rightly point out that, as explanations, these appeals go beyond the evidence and add nothing to our knowledge of the causes of the event. The truth of this is so easily acknowledged, however, that the fact that people nonetheless continue to make references to God and miracles should alert us to the possibility that the significance of their appeal may not have much to do with looking for explanations. Perhaps something quite different is going on when people call upon God. The conclusion seems to be that religious experience is not to be thought of along the same lines as everyday experience, and hence is not to be understood as merely more information to be used in the business of supplying evidence or giving explanations.

A second important consideration is this. In what has been said so far, we have assumed that religion underwrites values (if it does) by showing that God has issued explicit directions for the conduct of a good life. Now in one way this is true. But in another it is not. If we think, as many do, that religions lay down rules for a morally good life, or for a personally successful one, we have made an important mistake, because such a view, however common, is contrary to the facts about religious codes of conduct. Very little of what we find in the sacred literature of the world's religions is expressly to do with what might be called moral conduct, and even less with worldly success.

This is true of even the most familiar examples people use. Take the ten commandments. The first four of these have to do with our relationship to God, not relationships between people, and the remaining six take the larger part of their significance from this fact. Or consider the Sermon on the Mount. Though often spoken of as an elevating piece of moral teaching, the Sermon on the Mount is in fact much more concerned with how to pray and worship than it is with the details of ethical conduct. Again, the Qur'an has a great deal to say about how to keep in the right path ordained by God, but relatively little of this has to do with moral injunctions, and most of it with 'calling upon the Name'. The principal duties of the Muslim are prayer and worship. The same is true of the

Sikh scriptures. Even the Buddhist scriptures, though much concerned with how to live, are interested in the religious path to release from this world rather than rules for successful living in it. The fact is that the great religions of the world are not principally concerned with ethics at all, but with the religious life for its own sake. Their aim is not to make men and women good or successful, but to bring them into a relationship with the divine.

We might summarize these two points in this way. First, the springs of religion lie in experience that is not to be thought of as merely adding more to the general accumulation of evidence and formulation of explanations. Second, the sort of life religion recommends, though it may contain elements having to do with moral right and wrong and with personal happiness and achievement, is a distinctive *sort* of life. What both points suggest is that religious experience and conduct provide a context in which other sorts of human endeavour are to be assessed and understood. In religion we do not have a simple expansion of other concerns—scientific, moral, or personal—but a change of perspective. Religion, in a phrase of David F Swenson's, is a "transforming power of otherworldliness".

Neither of these considerations in itself provides convincing answers to the three major problems outlined. What they may do, however, is set us upon a line of thought that will eventually supply the means of answering them. We shall have to see. But in the meantime we can conclude that the importance of religion, if it has any, is not to supply better explanations of natural phenomena or underwrite the deliverances of morality more securely, but to provide a context in which these things are given *meaning*.

THE MYTH OF SISYPHUS

That religion is principally concerned with the meaning of life is almost a commonplace. But philosophers have found it difficult to determine just what is meant by 'meaning' in this context. 'Does life have a meaning?' is a question the meaningfulness of which may itself be doubted. In order to become a little clearer about the issues involved here, we can usefully explore the ancient myth of Sisyphus, especially as this has been illuminatingly elaborated by Richard Taylor.

Sisyphus was a legendary king of the ancient Greek city of Corinth. He was reputed to be exceedingly cunning, and amongst the most fantastical deeds attributed to him is the story that, when Death came to take him, Sisyphus managed to chain it up, so that no one died until Ares came and released Death again. In the end Sisyphus was condemned to eternal punishment for, amongst other misdeeds, betraying divine secrets to mortals. It is the form of his punishment that is of interest here. Sisyphus had to roll a large stone up a hillside. But things were so arranged that, just as the stone reached the top, it would tumble down to the bottom and he had to begin all over again. And so it would continue *forever*.

This story has always exercised considerable fascination. It has been embroidered in a number of different ways, and formed the subject matter of a well-known essay by the French existentialist writer Albert Camus. But however we embroider the myth, it is important to see that the labours of Sisyphus are not objectionable because they are difficult or tedious, but because they encapsulate a perfect image of *pointlessness*. Sisyphus's life, spent in the way the myth describes, is a meaningless one; this is what makes it a punishment. And the meaninglessness arises from the fact that he is trapped in an endless cycle of activity where what he does at one time (pushing the stone up the hill) is completely undone shortly after (when it rolls down again). It is the fact that nothing enduring is accomplished or attained that makes the whole thing pointless. Having seen that in this way Sisyphus's life is indeed meaningless, however, we are at the same time usefully placed to ask what would give it meaning.

Taylor suggests two possible modifications to the story. Suppose in their mercy the gods, though doing nothing to materially alter the task and conditions assigned to Sisyphus, inject him with a substance that has the curious property of giving him a desire to roll stones. As a result, when he is rolling the stone, however pointlessly, he is happy, and as the stone rolls down hill again, he grows restless and eager to begin his labours once more. This odd desire on Sisyphus's part is of course non-rational; it is, after all, merely the result of a substance injected into him. But for all that, it gives his activities a value for him, since the existence of the desire allows him a measure of satisfaction with the life to which he has been condemned. We might describe the position thus. Sisyphus's life has *subjective* value; it contains something that matters *to him*. However, it still has no meaning. The endless rolling of a worthless stone remains pointless. Nothing about the activity itself has changed. All that has changed is Sisyphus's attitude to it. And we might express this point by saying that, *objectively* speaking, there is no more meaning now than before.

But Taylor also invites us to consider a second modification in the story. Let us imagine that Sisyphus rolls not one stone but a series of stones to the top of the hill. This in itself does not alter the pointlessness of the activity. Now let us suppose that the stones that Sisyphus rolls have a key part to play in the construction of a gloriously beautiful temple. In this case all his strivings *do* have a point beyond the satisfaction of induced desires. They play a part in a project independent of the personal satisfaction of Sisyphus. We could express the difference by saying that, on this second modification of the story, Sisyphus's activity does come to have *objective* point or meaningfulness, because the facts about the activity, and not merely about Sisyphus, have been changed.

SUBJECTIVE VALUE AND OBJECTIVE MEANING

The distinction between subjective value and objective meaning is similar to one that we have encountered already, in the very first chapter in fact, and it has proved an important one in the examination of a number of the views we have considered. For this reason it is worth exploring a little further.

We can see in the case of Sisyphus that subjective value at best renders his activity meaningful in a very limited way. Having the strange desire he does may in the circumstances make him happier, and this no doubt is why Taylor describes it as an act of mercy on the part of the gods. But though the fact that he is pursuing his own happiness makes his activity more intelligible, the things he finds his happiness in still seem fruitless and silly. Indeed, given other modifications to the story, we can intelligibly pity this Sisyphus *more* than the first. Suppose he not only enjoys rolling stones, but believes it to be of the greatest importance. Unlike the old Sisyphus, who, though condemned, could at least shake his fist at the gods in recognition of what he had been condemned to, this new Sisyphus is not only condemned but *deluded*. He does not see the full extent of his condemnation.

Now consider objective meaning. Suppose it is true that the stones Sisyphus so laboriously pushes to the top of the hill are indeed crucial to the architectural glories of the heavens, but suppose at the same time that Sisyphus knows nothing of this. Then, though there is a point to what he does, he himself cannot see it. His existence and activity remain valueless for him. He can take no satisfaction in them and life will be, for him, as pointless a round of drudgery as it was before. It seems that neither the provision of subjective value nor objective meaning is alone sufficient to redeem the lot of Sisyphus. What is necessary is that some purpose or point is served by what he does, and that he knows and desires that this be the case. Only under these conditions can it be true that he has a fully meaningful existence.

What is true of the story of Sisyphus replicates a conclusion we have arrived at at some point in every chapter of this book. We saw that egoism was defective in part because it rested upon a divorce between the subjectively desired and the objectively desirable. Similarly, pleasure was insufficient as the touchstone of good because it too admitted the possibility that subjective pleasure and objective good be wholly separated. So, too, with existentialism, which tries to find objectivity in pure subjectivity. With Kantianism and utilitarianism, the fault lies in the other direction. Both erect systems of objective good and bad, right and wrong, but offer no explanation of how they might generate subjective value, i.e., value for those to whom they apply.

If this is correct, any adequate account of a meaningful life, and by extension, a good one, must provide a basis for both objective meaning and subjective value. Some philosophers have denied that this is possible. For instance, the American philosopher Thomas Nagel, in a well-known essay entitled "The Absurd", argues that the objective and subjective points of view are mutually exclusive. From this it follows that we cannot reasonably look for any means of uniting the two. But, Nagel goes on to argue, the felt need to do so is in any case a sort of confusion. Being creatures who are able to adopt a point of view that is objective with respect to subjective involvement, we are prone to a sense that life is absurd or meaningless. But we should worry about this only if we insist on mistakenly applying the objective point of view to things that can only admit of subjective value. Not surprisingly, they fail to meet the test—what is important to human beings cannot be shown to be important in some other more objective sense. According to Nagel, however, it does not need to be shown to be objectively important, since it is important in the only way that matters, namely subjectively.

Richard Taylor, whose amplification of the Sisyphus myth we have been following, does not think that objective and subjective meaning are in principle mutually exclusive. But he does think that subjective meaning is better, because objective meaning is unobtainable. To see why he thinks this we need to look at the story once more. On one modification, Sisyphus remains condemned to repeat an operation that results in nothing and is made to feel happy with his lot. On the other modification, his activity is given a point, its contribution to a magnificent temple. But if we think about this further, Taylor says, we see that, though of longer duration, the building of such temples is also subject to destruction. No matter how great a human achievement we consider—the Egyptian pyramids, Chinese civilization, or the Roman Empire—we know that the passage of time has eventually brought them to naught. In reality those activities we are inclined to rank as most valuable and enduring are no less part of a cycle of repeated creation and decay. What makes even them valuable is nothing more than the fact that we whose activities they are take a pride and satisfaction in them.

In other words, the modifications of the Sisyphus myth we have been exploring do not really present us with an alternative between subjective and objective value. Both make Sisyphus's life valuable and meaningful in *subjective* ways. Neither could lend it objective value, on Taylor's view, because nothing does endure for all eternity. Of course Taylor does not deny that the striving for objective meaning and value is a marked part of human life. He quotes the well-known Christian hymn:

> Change and decay in all around I see
> O Thou who changest not, abide in me

But Taylor contends that though a longing for unity with the eternal is a marked characteristic of human beings, it is ultimately in vain. Its satisfaction would have to lie in a world where 'there is neither pain or grief' but where, too, all strivings had ceased, and where, consequently, total boredom would overwhelm us. If there is one life worse than Sisyphus's, it is that in which nothing is done at all.

THE RELIGIOUS PERSPECTIVE

Both Nagel and Taylor, in different ways, reject an aspiration that may be said to inspire the belief that religion can provide a perspective within which we might hope to combine both objective meaning and subjective value. It should be observed straight away, however, that whether they are right or wrong in this, not all religions could provide such a perspective. The possibility of just such a perspective is precisely what Buddhism, for instance, denies. In common with other Eastern religions, Buddhism thinks of human beings as caught up in an inexorably turning wheel of existence and the thing that chains them to it is constant desire to be doing and achieving. This human desire or craving can never be wholly satisfied since with desire necessarily comes the possibility of privation and frustration.

The secret of religious enlightenment, revealed to the Buddha as he sat beneath the Boddhi tree, is the supression of desire, a systematic elimination of all our attachments to the world. In such turning away comes *moksha*, or release, and, eventually, for it may take more than one life to achieve it, entry to *Nirvana*—a term that captures both the idea of nothingness and of heaven. The Buddhist ideal, then, finds supreme value in personal extinction. (Whether this amounts to total extinction is a further matter.) In so doing, it wholly discounts subjective values—it is these after all that keep us chained to the unending round of birth, death, and rebirth. It is of great interest to note that, while Western minds are accustomed to think of religious faith entailing the belief and hope that we will be saved from eternal death and live forever, the belief of Eastern religions is that, other things being equal, we *do* live forever and it is from this dreadful fate that we must look to spirituality to save us.

It is only certain religions, then, that are likely to provide the sort of perspective for which we are looking, and chief among these are the great monotheistic religions of the West—Judaism, Christianity, and Islam. All three religions have a common root, namely the religion of the ancient Israelites. The essence of ancient Judaism is to be found in the Hebrew scriptures, and these begin, as is well known, with the book of Genesis, a word which means, of course, original creation.

It is very clear from the opening chapters of Genesis that its authors meant above all else to attribute to God the creation of *everything*; his creation was *ex nihilo*, from nothing. So, we are told, before creation began everything was "without form and void". It is also clear that as things come into existence the test of their adequacy is whether God regards them as good from the point of view of his creative purposes. God in effect *creates* good. A parallel with human creativity may be instructive here. When an accomplished artist paints a picture or a gifted composer writes a piece of music, the whole context of their work makes each part of it 'right' for the place in which it appears. Part of their genius is that they are able to construct sequences of sound or vision that are perfect in their place. But the perfection is not something independent of the work. It arises from the contribution that each part makes to the whole.

Similarly with divine creation. Any piece of God's handiwork takes its value from its place in the whole story of creation. When it comes to the creation of human beings we are told that man is made "in the image of God" and thus able to appreciate and use the good things that have been created. But, as is well known, creation is followed by the Fall, and the effect of this event is to rupture the unanimity between God and man, to introduce the possibility of divergence between the fundamental principles of creation and the mentality of human beings. The subsequent development of the three great monotheistic religions may reasonably be interpreted as an attempt to understand how this rupture might be repaired.

Whatever way we regard the creation story and its relation to contemporary science, whether as spiritual myth or primitive cosmology (or both), it is not difficult to see how it relates to the topics of this chapter. If God creates good *ex nihilo*, there is no sense in which it can be independent of his will. On the other hand, if human beings have the freedom to diverge from the principles of creation, we can easily conceive of circumstances in which they subjectively desire something different to what God's creative act intended for them. There is thus a sense in which what is objectively good and what is subjectively good come apart. The ideal condition, of course, is one in which human beings want for themselves what, by their very creation, God has ordained for them, and bringing this to pass is what talk of salvation and redemption is all about.

We need not concern ourselves here with the difficult matter of just how all this is to be understood, what truth there is in it, and what sense we can make of it. Our purpose has been to sketch in outline a religious perspective in order to see whether in principle it can solve those problems in the philosophy of value that the appeal to religion is meant to solve. To decide this question, we need to look again at the three difficulties set out earlier.

THE THREE DIFFICULTIES RECONSIDERED

These three difficulties were the problem of evil, the problem of religious knowledge, and the *Euthyphro* dilemma. To see how the sort of religious perspective just outlined might provide ways of overcoming these difficulties, it needs to be stressed at the outset that the fundamental conception of good at work is itself a religious one. From a religious point of view, the ultimate aim of all human thought and activity must be to return us to our proper place in creation and hence to a harmonious relationship with God, the source of everything.

For those who adopt it, this way of thinking throws a different light on the problem of evil. To begin with, though the things that we commonly describe as evils—pain, degradation, death—are indeed bad, evil properly speaking must now be thought of as those things that present obstacles to restoring the relationship with God. Pain and death *can* be evils for they may indeed create obstacles of this sort. People are often made bitter and resentful by their sufferings and the frustration of their hopes. But this is not *necessarily* so. As I observed earlier, not infrequently calamitous events can prompt religious belief, often by engendering a sense of total dependence, and sometimes we can overcome the evil things that happen to us by gracefully accepting them. Literature is full of stories the point of which is to show how the same material suffering (war, for instance) destroyed one person while raising another to almost superhuman heights.

Second, if we adopt the religious perspective, we have to understand the idea of the love of God somewhat differently from the idea assumed by the normal version of the problem of evil. To say that God is infinitely loving means that he wants and is always ready to grant a relationship of communion—being at one—with his creatures. To question the reality of God's unfailing love, then, is to doubt whether he really does want such a relationship with his creation. But if the first point about evil is correctly taken, we cannot properly conclude that the existence of evils in the ordinary everyday sense is indeed evidence against the love of God. A proper relationship with the divine is not easily secured, no doubt, but to show that God does not love us we would have to show that there are contexts and occasions on which it is *impossible*, and this is what the existence of death, degradation, and suffering on their own *cannot* show. So long as it is true that these things can be overcome, they do not constitute evidence against the love of God.

From a religious perspective, the problem of evil, then, is not what it is commonly made out to be. This does not make death, destruction, and so on, any easier to tolerate, of course. The question 'Where was God in the Holocaust?' is still an important and deeply troubling one from a religious point of view, insofar as we cannot imagine how God might be sought and found by the victims or perpetrators. But the answer to the problem, if there is one, could not consist in any kind of mitigation or explaining away of that horrendous period of history. Rather, religious reflection must show, if it can, how even horrors of that magnitude may be overcome.

An appeal to the religious perspective also casts a different light on the problem of religious knowledge. Certainly it is true that the prescriptions for human conduct that religious teachers have made differ considerably. But it seems broadly correct to say that they are all to be characterized as the removal of obstacles to restoring a right relationship with God. They thus share the same aim. About just how this aim is to be accomplished they differ, but their differing in this respect is philosophically speaking no more significant than differences between scientists and historians over which are the right research methods to use.

It is true that in many instances religious differences are much more fundamental than this parallel suggests, but then, presumably, the religious quest is a much more ambitious one than the scientific. There is not space here to go into the matter fully, but before we can assume that religious differences (unlike scientific ones) are ultimately irresolvable, it needs to be shown that there has been no progress in religious understanding in any way comparable to that in scientific understanding, and that we never have good reason to abandon religious doctrines and prescriptions which were formerly widely accepted. For my part I do not think this can be shown. If that is right, we can say that the great variety of religious doctrine and prescription, though it presents practical difficulties, does not in itself represent a philosophical objection to the idea of religious knowledge.

The problem of religious knowledge led on to the *Euthyphro* dilemma by suggesting that in trying to sort out the competing claims for different religions we have no choice but to turn to other more familiar standards of good and bad. Now we can see this to be a mistake. There is indeed a *religious* standard by which they are to be judged, namely, the adequacy of each religious prescription to remove real obstacles to a relationship with the divine. There is, however, a problem of another sort here. We can state this test in the abstract. But how are we to know when it has been satisfied? To my mind, the answer to this question can only lie with an appeal to the religious experience of humankind. The proper test for recommendations for the religious life must take the form of assessing whether they properly encapsulate what both ordinary believers and mystics have said and felt and whether they really do open up avenues to such experiences. It needs to be said at once, of course, that many people think religious experience to be illusory and the believer and mystic to be deluded. These are important claims and need to be investigated, but once more this is not a topic that can be entered into further here.

What is important for present purposes is to see that the appeal to a religious perspective does not answer the *Euthyphro* dilemma by providing reason to opt for one horn rather than the other. Rather, it supplies a different conception of good in the light of which the relative importance of those things which we generally regard as good and bad may be assessed. Consider again a parallel with human creativity—this time, the writing of a play. Imagine a play of which there survive, apparently, only fragmentary portions. The play as a whole is lost, but people nevertheless perform and enjoy the fragments and have their own estimates of the respective merits of the characters and events they contain. From time to time another fragment is discovered, but one day the text of the whole play is found. This throws a completely new light upon our understanding of the fragments we already possessed. Moreover, it does so in a different way to the acquisition of one more fragment because it reveals to us the plot and hence the meaning of the play. In turn this brings about a re-estimation of the older fragments. They do not lose the capacity to give enjoyment, but this is tempered now by an understanding of their relative importance in the work as a whole.

The parallel is this. We have seen that in thinking about the good life there is a sort of fragmentation between the claims of personal happiness and fulfilment and the claims of impartial respect for the good of others. We can see that both matter, but cannot quite see how they can be put together. The problem with those secular philosophies examined in the first five chapters is that none of them seems able to supply an answer. Within the religious perspective, however, we can see how one might be provided. Both personal happiness and morally decent conduct towards others have their part to play in re-establishing communion with the divine. Neither, however, is to be identified with that aim, and neither is to be regarded as good independently of the contribution it makes to that communion. In what theologians call 'the divine economy', both personal happiness and respect for others are important, but they take their importance, and their relative importance, from their place in the task of redemption.

THE UNITY OF THE OBJECTIVE AND SUBJECTIVE: 'WHERE TRUE JOYS ARE TO BE FOUND'

We can also see how the appeal to religion might be thought to overcome the tension between subjective value and objective meaning. It is true that there is a divinely ordained purpose that explains both the nature and the meaning of the cosmos (objective meaning). Its fulfilment requires human participation, and this implies, among other things, rules for the conduct of human relations. It is also true, however, that fulfilment of God's purpose is possible only with the willing co-operation of human beings and that accordingly men and women have been given free will. This, on the other hand, allows them to diverge from God's ordination if they so choose. Given the creation of all things together, ultimately the most satisfactory world is one in which human beings come to follow, subjectively, the divinely prescribed order, and hence find greatest value in the divine purpose. In this way, in a familiar phrase, the service of God is perfect freedom. Within the religious perspective, total subservience to God is the condition of human freedom from sin and death. Religious subservience of this sort is the whole aim of Islam, a word actually meaning 'submission', whose devotee is called a 'muslim', the one who follows 'the straight path'. It is also a religious aspiration marvellously expressed in this old Christian prayer.

Almighty God, who alone canst order the unruly wills and affections of sinful men: Grant unto thy people, that they may love the thing which thou commandest, and desire that which thou dost promise; that so, among the great and many changes of the world, our hearts may surely there be fixed, where true joys are to be found.

Such at any rate is one view of the religious perspective and of the way in which it overcomes some of the difficulties encountered in earlier chapters. Unfortunately, if it does solve some problems, it brings others no less serious in its wake. One of these is the sheer difficulty of religious thought and language. For many, religious 'insight' is accomplished only by trading in mystery mongering. Religious theorizing for them is a good case of *obscurum per obscurius*—explaining the obscure by means of the more obscure. This is not always so, but even when religious language does not seem impossibly difficult to attach sense to, religious thought necessitates a great deal of metaphysical theorising, about the relation of God to the world for instance, and it calls into play whole worlds beyond our ordinary perception. Consequently, the value of such resolutions of problems in the philosophy of the good life as an appeal to religion may offer is offset by the further problems it raises.

More important, religious belief arises not merely from intellectual inquiry and speculation, but from religious feeling and experience. It is rarely, if ever, that people are argued into religious conviction. Without this crucial element, religious ideas remain, so to speak, inanimate, and the theoretical problems they engender seem little more than intellectual curiosities. The appeal to religion, therefore, cannot be successful on the basis of philosophical argument alone. Moreover, the philosophical exploration of religious ideas is very unwelcome to many religious people, who would rather rely upon the authority of a church or on personal 'faith'. It is true that the origins of much contemporary intellectual inquiry lie with the Christian religion, but it is also true that the history of religion, including Christianity, contains a good deal of hostility to intellectual criticism. From both points of view, that of secular scepticism and of unreflective religion, the ideas of this final chapter do not present viable solutions. For those who take either view, religion cannot and should not be expected to complete a philosophical task and the argument proper must be regarded as having ended with the last chapter.

For some, then, religious faith may provide further avenues of exploration for the issues we have been concerned with. For others, it cannot. But if we were to return to the end of the last chapter and stop there, a serious problem remains. How are the egoistic demands of personal happiness and the altruistic demands of morality to be squared? To ask this question is to ask whether there is *a* good life. Is it not rather the case that the morally virtuous life and the personally happy one are radically *different* conceptions of the good life? But, if so, which should we choose, and how are conflicts between them to be resolved?

The recourse to religious ideas is intended to overcome such conflicts, but it brings with it ideas that are difficult to make sense of. Those who take the view that the ideas invoked by religion are too abstruse and perplexing to provide much illumination, and lack the sort of religious feeling that prompts people to persist with them, face the following choices. First, they could somehow learn to live with the dichotomy. This is what the majority of people do, in fact. They pay *most* attention to personal concerns and *some* attention to what they perceive to be moral demands. Such people get by, but their mode of existence is unsatisfactory from a philosophical point of view, since it is deeply incoherent. But then, they may not worry about philosophy.

For those to whom philosophical reflections matter, a second option presents itself—to opt for one conception or the other, in the way that Kant opts for the deliverances of pure practical reason. The objection to this alternative, however, is that all the arguments appear to have shown neither option to be wholly satisfactory in itself.

The arguments *appear* to show this, but is it true? This raises a third possibility, that the arguments be examined all over again, that we go back to the start and reconsider the questions of moral philosophy as critically as we can. To arrive at the end of a book and reach this result may initially be dispiriting. Can the whole thing have been worthwhile? Yet this third option is in fact the properly philosophical one, and the one best warranted by the book itself. Those who have been caught up in the arguments will have seen very clearly that there are countless issues here that need to be explored again and again. Philosophy is a large and ancient subject. Though the book is full of conclusions, it is properly named—an *introduction* to moral philosophy.

SUGGESTED FURTHER READING

Original Sources
Plato, *Euthyphro*
David Hume, *Dialogues concerning Natural Religion*
J S Mill, *Three Essays on Religion*

Contemporary Discussion
R Campbell and D Collinson, *Ending Lives*, chap. 3
P T Geach, *God and the Soul*
E D Klemke (ed.), *The Meaning of Life*

BIBLIOGRAPHY

This list contains publication details of all books and essays quoted from or referred to in the text and suggested further reading.

Aristotle
Nicomachean Ethics
trans. Sir David Ross
Worlds Classics, Oxford University
Press
Oxford, 1925

Jeremy Bentham
A Fragment on Government and
*Introduction to the Principles of Morals
and Legislation*
ed. Wilfred Harrison, Basil Blackwell
Oxford, 1960

R Campbell and
D Collinson
Ending Lives, Basil Blackwell
Oxford, 1988

Arthur C Danto
Sartre
Fontana Modern Masters, Collins
Glasgow, 1975

Charles Dickens
Oliver Twist
Worlds Classics, Oxford University
Press
Oxford, 1966

Patrick Gardiner

Kierkegaard
Past Masters, Oxford University Press
Oxford, 1988

David Gautier

Morals by Agreement,
Clarendon Press
Oxford, 1986

Peter Geach

God and the Soul, Routledge
London, 1969

William Godwin

Enquiry Concerning Political Justice
ed. and abridged K.C. Carter,
Clarendon Press, Oxford 1971

Oswald Hanfling

The Quest for Meaning, Basil Blackwell
Oxford, 1988

Jonathan Harrison

Hume's Moral Epistemology,
Clarendon Press
Oxford, 1976

G W F Hegel

The Philosophy of Right,
trans. T M Knox
Clarendon Press
Oxford, 1952

Christopher Hibbert

*The Personal History of Samuel
Johnson*, Penguin
London, 1971

R J Hollingdale

*Nietzsche: The Man and His
Philosophy*, Routledge
London, 1985

David Hume

Dialogues concerning Natural Religion,
ed. Norman Kemp Smith
Macmillan, London, 1947

A Treatise of Human Nature
3rd edition, ed. P H Nidditch,
Clarendon Press
Oxford, 1975

Francis Hutcheson

Inquiry into the Original of Our Ideas of Beauty and Virtue
ed. Peter Kivy, Nijhoff,
The Hague, 1973

Terence Irwin

Plato's Moral Theory,
Oxford University Press,
Oxford, 1977.

Immanuel Kant

Foundations of the Metaphysics of Morals
trans. Lewis White Beck, Bobbs Merrill
Indianapolis, 1959

Walter Kaufman

Nietzsche: Philosopher, Psychologist, Anti-Christ
3rd edition, Princeton University Press
Princeton, 1968

Søren Kierkegaard

Concluding Unscientific Postscript
trans. D Swenson and W Lowrie,
Princeton University Press
Princeton, 1968

Journals
ed. Alexander Dru
London, 1938

E D Klemke (ed.)

The Meaning of Life, Oxford University Press
New York, 1981

Diogenes Laertius

Lives of the Philosophers
trans. R D Hicks
Heinemann, London 1925

A A Long and
D N Sedley

The Hellenistic Philosophers, vol. 1
Cambridge, 1987

Konrad Lorenz

On Aggression
London, 1963

David Lyons

Forms and Limits of Utilitarianism,
Clarendon Press
Oxford, 1965

Alasdair MacIntyre

Against the Self-Images of the Age,
Duckworth
London, 1971

After Virtue, Duckworth
London, 1981

A Short History of Ethics, Routledge
London, 1967

John MacQuarrie

Existentialism, Hutchinson
London, 1972

Anthony Manser

Sartre, Athlone Press,
London, 1966

Mary Midgely

Beast and Man, Methuen
London, 1978

John Stuart Mill

Utilitarianism, ed. Mary Warnock
Collins
London, 1962

	Three Essays on Religion Collected Works, vol. 10, ed. J M Robson Toronto, 1969
Desmond Morris	*The Naked Ape*, Corgi London, 1967
Thomas Nagel	*The Possibility of Altruism* Clarendon Press, Oxford, 1970
Friedrich Neitzsche	*Twilight of the Idols* and *The Anti-Christ* trans. R J Hollingdale Penguin Classics London, 1968
H J Paton	*The Categorical Imperative*, Hutchinson, London 1947
D Z Phillips (ed.)	*Religion and Understanding*, Basil Blackwell Oxford, 1967
Plato	*Euthyphro*, in *Dialogues of Plato Vol. 1* trans. Benjamin Jowett Clarendon Press Oxford, 1970
	The Gorgias trans. Walter Hamilton Penguin Classics London, 1960
	The Republic trans. Desmond Lee Penguin Classics London, 1955

Anthony Quinton

Utilitarian Ethics, Macmillan
London, 1973

Jean Paul Sartre

Being and Nothingness
trans. Hazel Barnes, Methuen
London, 1958

Existentialism and Humanism
trans. Philip Mairet, Methuen
London, 1973

J J C Smart and
B Williams

Utilitarianism for and against,
Cambridge University Press
Cambridge, 1973

Robert C Solomon

Continental Philosophy since 1750
History of Western Philosophy, Vol. 7,
Oxford University Press
Oxford, 1988

Frederick Sontag

A Kierkegaard Workbook
John Knox Press
Atlanta, 1979

Richard Taylor

Good and Evil
Prometheus New York, 1970

J O Urmson

Aristotle's Ethics,
Clarendon Press
Oxford, 1988

Bernard Williams

Ethics and the Limits of Philosophy,
Collins
London, 1985

Peter Winch

Ethics and Action, Routledge
London, 1972

INDEX

DATE DUE

DEMCO